DK GARDEN GUIDES

FUCHSIAS

RICHARD BIRD

LONDON, NEW YORK,
MUNICH, MELBOURNE, DELHI

Series Editor Zia Allaway
Series Art Editor Alison Donovan
Art Editor Ann Thompson
Editor Christine Dyer
Managing Editor Anna Kruger
Managing Art Editor Lee Griffiths
Consultants Louise Abbott, Roger Gilbert
DTP Designer Louise Waller
Media Resources Richard Dabb, Lucy Claxton
Picture Research Juliet Duff
Production Controller Mandy Inness
US Editor Christine Heilman
US Senior Editor Jill Hamilton
US Editorial Assistant John Searcy

Additional Text Christine Dyer
Introduction Text Zia Allaway

First American Edition, 2003

Published in the United States by
DK Publishing, Inc.
375 Hudson Street
New York, New York 10014

01 02 03 04 05 10 9 8 7 6 5 4 3 2 1

A Cataloging-in-Publication record for this book
is available from the Library of Congress.

ISBN 0-7894-9343-8

Color reproduction by Colourscan, Singapore
Printed and bound in Italy by Printer Trento

discover more at
www.dk.com

Gardening with fuchsias

I T'S DIFFICULT TO PINPOINT the exact reason why fuchsias are so popular with gardeners and have remained firm favorites since Victorian times. Perhaps it's their dainty flowers, suspended from delicate arching stems like tiny pirouetting ballerinas, or the fact that many are easy to grow and return a dazzling performance of flowers and foliage from late spring to the first frost in autumn. They're adaptable too, with compact, tender types making perfect partners for annual bedding in pots and baskets, while in mild areas, large bush fuchsias can be used to create superb flowering hedges that will reach up to head-height.

Fuchsias fall broadly into two groups: the half-hardy and tender varieties, which include those with the largest and most flamboyant flowers, and the hardy fuchsias that will survive the winter in mild regions and generally have smaller blooms. The flowers within both groups come in a vast range of shapes and sizes: double, frilly-skirted blooms, long, slender, tubelike flowers, and even those, such as *Fuchsia procumbens*, with flowers that face upward. There is also a huge choice of colors, from pure white, clear pink, and peachy orange to deep red and dark purple, plus stunning combinations of contrasting shades.

◀ **Triphylla fuchsias** have elegant, long tubular flowers and make excellent feature plants.

▶ **'Pink Galore' describes** perfectly the warm tones of this classic trailing fuchsia.

Dazzling foliage

The showy flowers are reason enough to grow fuchsias, but some types match beautiful blooms with eye-catching foliage. The lime-yellow leaves of 'Genii' will brighten up a lightly shaded border as soon as they unfurl in spring and, when set against the cerise and violet flowers, the effect is magical. Others with colorful foliage include *F. magellanica* var. *gracilis* 'Tricolor', which has variegated leaves tinged with pink veining, and 'Strawberry Delight' with its pale green and bronze foliage.

White fuchsias cool any color scheme, and look particularly effective when mixed with pink and purple.

Combine pots filled with fuchsias and annuals to create a colorful display.

Pots and patios

The versatility of fuchsias makes them excellent choices for any patio or balcony display. Trailing types, such as 'Auntie Jinks' or 'Red Spider', with their cascading stems and profusion of flowers, are perfect for hanging baskets and window boxes, while a bushy fuchsia, such as the elegant white and red 'Checkerboard', is shown off to best effect when planted in a simple terracotta pot. Those with sturdy upright stems, such as 'Celia Smedley' and 'Thalia', are easy to train into standards and other shapes.

Planting plans

The easiest way to grow fuchsias is in a bed or border, simply because any plant grown in a pot requires more feeding and watering than one

Big and bold, hardy fuchsias need little care, except for a blanket of bark chips over their crowns in winter.

Sizzling summer borders are fired up with the hot flower colors and vivid foliage of this hardy fuchsia.

Tender care

Tender and half-hardy fuchsias must be brought into a heated greenhouse, a cool, unheated room or conservatory, or a bright, frost-free garage before the first frosts in autumn. Don't be tempted to bring your fuchsias into the house to overwinter, since the warm, dry air in a centrally heated home is not the most suitable environment for them.

This book offers an indispensable guide to fuchsias and covers a huge range of plants, many of which are available at garden centers. The list of specialist fuchsia nurseries at the back will help you to track down the more unusual varieties.

planted in the open ground. Tender fuchsias that flower for many months are ideal for filling gaps between more permanent plantings, and offer long-lasting interest. Taller hardy fuchsias, with their small flowers and lush foliage, are excellent foils for flowering annuals and perennials, or use them in a mixed shrub display.

To grow fuchsias as hedges, you need a mild climate where temperatures don't regularly dip too far below freezing. In these conditions, fuchsia hedges will thrive, making beautiful boundaries and natural divisions within the garden.

Wooden planters filled with fuchsias and ivy can be used to flank a front door, or as a focal point on a patio or at the end of a path.

Fuchsia flowers and habits

WHEN SELECTING FUCHSIAS, you may find it helpful to know which flower parts are referred to in the descriptions. The flowers come in many forms. Single fuchsias have four petals, semidoubles produce five to seven, and full doubles have eight or more. The Triphylla's long, tubelike blooms set them apart from the rest.

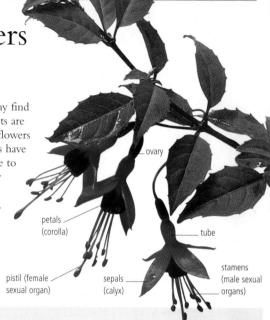

ovary

petals (corolla)

tube

pistil (female sexual organ)

sepals (calyx)

stamens (male sexual organs)

Parts of a fuchsia
The corolla, a term frequently used in fuchsia descriptions, refers to the petals, while the calyx is formed of sepals that protect the bud.

Different habits

Fuchsias fall into two main types, bush and trailing, which describe the shape and habit of the plant. Some fuchsias are also referred to as self-branching. This means that the stems divide automatically as they grow, resulting in a bushy fuchsia with a dense network of leafy shoots.

Bush fuchsias
Stiff stems and dense growth give bushes a good upright shape, ideal for containers or beds and borders.

Trailing fuchsias
The lax, flexible stems of these fuchsias are perfect for hanging baskets, window boxes, and tall pots.

Planting fuchsias in containers

YOUNG FUCHSIAS ARE EASILY DAMAGED when transplanted into large planters or containers. To prevent this, tip the fuchsias out of their original pots and use the pots to gauge space and planting depths before moving the plants themselves into position in the planter.

Fuchsias in containers

Before planting, water the fuchsias thoroughly in their pots. Then put pebbles or pieces of styrofoam in the bottom of the planter, and top it off with good-quality potting mix with added horticultural sand to improve drainage. This mix will help to ensure a good flower display. You can also add some water-retaining gel to the compost if the planter is going to stand in full sun.

1 Position the standard
Make sure the largest fuchsia will be at least 4in (10cm) below the top of the planter, giving enough of a gap to water the plants.

2 Finishing off
Place the pots of smaller fuchsias where required. Fill in around the pots with soil. Remove pots and put in the fuchsias, firming them in gently. Water well.

Caring for your fuchsias

MANY FUCHSIAS ARE EASY TO GROW, but all will give their best performance when given a little extra care. Water during dry spells and extend the flowering period by deadheading regularly.

Feeding and watering

Regular feeding with a balanced fertilizer will help your fuchsias produce strong growth and lots of flowers. Feed weekly or, as many experts advise, each time you water. If you do this, dilute the feed to a quarter of the usual strength and flush excess nutrients out of the soil once a week with plain water.

When to water
Water container-grown fuchsias when the top of the compost feels dry. Make sure water can drain easily from the pot—fuchsias hate wet soil.

Deadheading

Removing flowers as they fade both improves the appearance of your fuchsias and prevents them from putting energy into producing seeds instead of flower buds. If left, the plant may stop flowering altogether. Also, remove diseased leaves that may fall on, and contaminate, the soil.

Removing faded flowers
Never pull off spent flowers; instead, pinch them off at the base of the flower stem as shown.

Promoting spring growth

Hardy fuchsias flower on the current year's growth and, by pruning a plant hard in spring, you will encourage new, vigorous flowering shoots to develop. Even if buds appear on last year's stems, you should still cut back most of the old wood. Feed the plant after pruning to kick-start it into growth.

Spring pruning
In spring, cut back old growth or any that has been damaged by frost to encourage healthy, new stems to develop.

Taking fuchsia cuttings

FUCHSIAS ARE EASY to propagate when given warmth and moisture to stimulate new roots and shoots to develop. The best ways to raise new plants is to take soft-tip cuttings (below) in spring or autumn, as the seed of named fuchsias rarely produces plants as good as the parent. For the perfect soil mix, blend equal measures of peat substitute and sharp sand or vermiculite, although fuchsias root so easily that you can just pop them into a jar of water. A heated propagator will keep the cuttings warm and moist, but any sealed transparent container, such as a pickle jar, will do. Then wait for two or three weeks, during which time your cuttings should have rooted.

1 Remove a stem tip
Take cuttings from a healthy plant. Use a sharp knife to remove the growing tip of a young stem. Cut just above the second pair of mature leaves. Hold by a leaf.

— A soft-tip cutting with one set of mature leaves

2 Trim the leaves
To prevent cuttings from losing too much moisture through the foliage, trim off the tips of large leaves.

3 Plant the cuttings
Fill a tray or modules with moist soil mix (see above). Make a hole in the soil and insert the cutting. Do not allow the leaves to overlap.

4 Place in a propagator
Water the cuttings with a watering can with a fine nozzle. Label and put in a propagator or cover with plastic or glass. Keep in a shady, cool place, ideally at 60°F (16°C). New shoots will soon appear.

Training fuchsias

IT'S EASY TO TRAIN FUCHSIAS into compact bushy shapes or tall elegant standards, ideal for ornamental containers on a patio. You don't need any special equipment either, since most training simply involves pinching out young shoots with your fingers.

Pinch pruning bush fuchsias

Use the same method for pruning all of your bush fuchsias, whether you plan to use them in pots or in a border. Referred to as "pinching out," the tips of young shoots are nipped off in spring and early summer. This encourages the stems to divide and creates a bushy plant.

1 Remove the growing tip
Pinch out the top shoot of young plants to encourage sideshoots to grow.

2 Pinch out sideshoots
After a few weeks, pinch out the tips of the new sideshoots to produce even more bushy growth.

3 Final pinching
Repeat this process and then leave the plant to grow. Flowers will appear within 8–10 weeks.

Fan training
This fuchsia has been pinched out as shown above. The sideshoots have then been trained along short canes to produce a fan shape. This method is best used for fuchsias planted on their own as features in containers.

Training a standard fuchsia

Many fuchsias can be trained as standards. Look for young plants with a good strong main stem. If training fuchsias that have been grown from cuttings (see p.11), keep them warm and well lit throughout winter to give them a head start in spring. Feed in spring with a balanced fertilizer.

1 Pinch out shoots
Remove sideshoots that appear just above the leaf joints. Insert a stake and tie in the stem.

2 Remove sideshoots
Pinch out sideshoots regularly, but retain all the leaves on the stem. Repot and restake the plant.

3 Remove top shoot
When the fuchsia is about three sets of leaves taller than you require, pinch out the top shoot.

4 Pinch out tips
Pinch out the tips of the sideshoots growing at the top of the plant. Continue until the head thickens up.

Finishing off
When you have created a bushy head, remove all the leaves growing up the main stem, leaving it clear, as shown. Keep the plant staked, and repot as required.

A-Z of Fuchsias

A

'Abbé Farges'

WITH ITS UPRIGHT GROWTH and vigorous, branching habit,
'Abbé Farges' makes a very good standard, although it should
be handled with care because the stems are rather brittle and
have a reputation for snapping easily. Introduced in France in
1901, it remains popular today due to the abundance of small
flowers that are produced during summer. If you grow it as a
standard, you will need to provide adequate support and
choose a sheltered site where it will be protected from strong
winds. The daintiness of this fuchsia also makes it suitable for
treatment as a bonsai.

PLANT PROFILE

HEIGHT 18in (45cm)

SPREAD 12in (30cm)

HABIT Upright bush,
self-branching

HARDINESS Fully hardy

FLOWERING Summer to autumn

'Achievement'

A

HIGHLY RATED BY FUCHSIA EXPERTS, upright and bushy 'Achievement' is easy to grow and hardy enough to be left in the border year-round in warmer regions. An early and relentless flowerer, it guarantees a good show throughout summer. In a "hot" border, it will keep the flow of reds going, while among a collection of soft, pale-colored flowers, it would look fabulous as foreground interest.

PLANT PROFILE

HEIGHT 24–30in (60–75cm)

SPREAD 24–30in (60–75cm)

HABIT Upright bush, self-branching

HARDINESS Fully hardy

FLOWERING Summer to autumn

A | 'Alice Hoffman'

BUSHY, UPRIGHT, AND FREE-FLOWERING over a long period, the small, semidouble flowers of 'Alice Hoffman' provide a good color contrast—the tubes and sepals are rose pink, while the white corollas carry rose pink veining. The foliage is equally handsome, with dense clusters of small, bronze-tinged leaves covering the compact bush. In mild areas, if given a precautionary protective mulch of shredded bark, it can be left outdoors over winter. A neat, nonsprawling shape makes this cultivar a good choice for containers or rock gardens, or as a subject for bonsai.

PLANT PROFILE

HEIGHT 18–24in (45–60cm)

SPREAD 18–24in (45–60cm)

HABIT Compact, upright bush

HARDINESS Z9–11 H12–9

FLOWERING Summer to autumn

'Alison Patricia'

A RELATIVELY RECENT INTRODUCTION (1990), this bedding plant puts on plenty of growth early in the season. Its upward-shooting stems are liberally covered with semidouble flowers, making it an exceptional subject for containers, and creating a wonderful display when teamed with trailing foliage plants. Although 'Alison Patricia' can be grown in full sun, the colors stand out best in dappled shade.

PLANT PROFILE

HEIGHT 9–10in (23–25cm)

SPREAD 6–9in (15–23cm)

HABIT Upright bush

HARDINESS Half hardy

FLOWERING Summer to first frost

A | *alpestris*

A WILD, BUSHY FUCHSIA FROM BRAZIL, *F. alpestris* has some rather unusual features. Its small flowers have horizontal sepals that look like the long, thin wings of a hovering insect, while the corolla is tightly scrunched. The leaves are worthy of note too, with a red central vein and margin, and a covering of downy fuzz. With a growth habit that is best described as bordering on rampant, this isn't a plant for a crowded bed; it will be happiest climbing up a sunny wall where the stunning flowers can be seen to best effect. Rather confusingly, *F. alpestris* is often listed as *F. regia* var. *alpestris*.

PLANT PROFILE

HEIGHT 4–6ft (1.2–2m)

SPREAD 6–9ft (2–2.7m)

HABIT Upright, climbing

HARDINESS Half hardy

FLOWERING Summer to first frost

'Ambassador'

A

A PERFECT POT PLANT, 'Ambassador' has strong, upright, bushy growth with stems liberally sprinkled with very large, single flowers. It is a satisfyingly fast-growing cultivar. The tube and sepals are pink with white, while the corolla opens to dark violet, fading with age to light purple. More a chorus player than a headliner, it is best as a backdrop for other more vibrant fuchsias. In an ornamental herb garden it will add a touch of restrained color.

PLANT PROFILE	
HEIGHT 18–24in (45–60cm)	
SPREAD 15–18in (38–45cm)	
HABIT Upright bush, self-branching	
HARDINESS Half hardy	
FLOWERING Summer to first frost	

A   'Amelie Aubin'

STRONG-GROWING AND RELIABLE—just the qualities a novice gardener should be looking for—this unfussy fuchsia has large, elegant, single flowers that are a not-too-flamboyant mix of white and red. The stems are lax and have a trailing habit, making it a good choice for a hanging basket. In this elevated position, you will be able to glance up and enjoy a close-up of the flowers—the sepals are especially pretty, being rose tinted with green tips. If grown as a bush, regularly pinch out the growing tips to thicken it up and, unless the site is very sheltered, stake it securely.

PLANT PROFILE	
HEIGHT 18–24in (45–60cm)	
SPREAD 18–24in (45–60cm)	
HABIT Trailing	
HARDINESS Half hardy	
FLOWERING Summer to first frost	

'Amy Lye'

A

IDEAL FOR TRAINING AS A TRAILING STANDARD or pillar, the height and spreading habit of this fuchsia also give it a strong presence in the summer border. Regularly nipping out the growing tips, starting when the plant is young, will encourage a more abundant show of flowers and a bushy shape. Choose a spot for it in dappled shade, rather than full sun, to retain the petal color. The flowers feature the creamy white, waxy sepals and tube that are the trademark of the Victorian grower James Lye. Many of his most popular fuchsias carry this delicate coloration.

PLANT PROFILE

HEIGHT 18–24in (45–60cm)

SPREAD 15–18in (38–45cm)

HABIT Spreading, lax bush

HARDINESS Half hardy

FLOWERING Early summer to first frost

A | 'Andrew Hadfield'

IN TERMS OF BLOOMS PER SQUARE INCH, this upright shrub
is a bargain, with barely a stem that isn't packed with single
flowers. If the stems start to arch over with the weight, insert
canes to prevent them from snapping. The strong red sepals
and tube are toned down by a lilac-blue, open-shaped corolla
that carries pink veining and is white at the base. This cultivar
would make a colorful subject for a container or large
windowbox. For the best flower color, plant in dappled shade
and bring it under cover for the winter.

PLANT PROFILE	
HEIGHT 12–15in (30–38cm)	
SPREAD 9–12in (23–30cm)	
HABIT Upright bush	
HARDINESS Frost tender	
FLOWERING Summer to first frost	

'Anita'

A BRIGHTLY COLORED FUCHSIA introduced from Germany in 1989, 'Anita' is an unusual combination of clear white tube and sepals with a strong tangerine corolla. It is very easy to grow and the flowers, borne in profusion, are semierect. To retain a neat, upright, bushy shape, you will need to nip out the growing tips on a regular basis. If pot-grown outdoors, bring it under cover during the winter.

PLANT PROFILE	
HEIGHT 18–24in (45–60cm)	
SPREAD 15–18in (38–45cm)	
HABIT Strong, upright bush	
HARDINESS Half hardy	
FLOWERING Summer to first frost	

A | 'Annabel'

A TOP-QUALITY, UPRIGHT PLANT that can be grown in the border, in hanging baskets, or trained as a pillar or standard. Since it was introduced in 1977, its prolific displays of large, double flowers—predominantly white but flushed with pink—have endeared it to many gardeners. Although the stems tend to be lax, they are strong enough to carry the loose clusters of heavy blooms. Take care when handling the buds because they bruise easily. The foliage is light to mid-green. Choose a spot away from bright sun to protect the petal color.

PLANT PROFILE

HEIGHT 12–24in (30–60cm)

SPREAD 12–24in (30–60cm)

HABIT Lax bush, self-branching

HARDINESS Z9–11 H12–9

FLOWERING Summer to first frost

'Annabelle Stubbs'

A

TO TRACK DOWN THIS FUCHSIA you may have to go to a specialist nursery, but it is well worth the effort, especially if you want something spectacular for a hanging basket. An American introduction from 1991, 'Annabelle Stubbs' has lax stems that have a natural tendency to trail. A strong combination of light pink tube, coral sepals, and red-purple corolla makes an eye-catching centerpiece for any planting plan.

PLANT PROFILE

HEIGHT 15–18in (38–45cm)

SPREAD 15–18in (38–45cm)

HABIT Trailing

HARDINESS Half hardy

FLOWERING Summer to first frost

A 'Ann Howard Tripp'

NOT ONE FOR THE BEGINNER, this fuchsia—sometimes listed under the abbreviated name of 'Ann H. Tripp'—is often tricky to keep over winter. It is also slow to start flowering, but when it gets going, it produces masses of dainty, single to semidouble white blooms that are suffused with the palest pink. Two flowers are produced in each leaf axil (where the leaf joins the stem). The leaves are yellow when new but turn pale green as they mature. Bushy and upright in habit, it makes a good bedding plant. For the best blooms, protect it from heavy rain, which may mark the petals, and keep it out of bright sunlight.

PLANT PROFILE

HEIGHT 6–9in (15–23cm)

SPREAD 6–9in (15–23cm)

HABIT Upright bush, self-branching

HARDINESS Half hardy

FLOWERING Summer to first frost

arborescens Lilac fuchsia

A

THE EVERGREEN LILAC FUCHSIA is a wonderful, unfuchsialike curiosity. It has large, lustrous, green leaves and, in a few weeks over summer, produces one flush of small, open, lilaclike flowers. These are followed by round, purple fruits. Originally from Mexico, it is best grown in a cool conservatory, although in summer it can be moved to a sunny but sheltered spot in the garden. Plant it in a large pot to give it a good root run and encourage plenty of topgrowth. Good drainage is essential, but the potting mix must never be allowed to dry out.

PLANT PROFILE

HEIGHT 6ft (2m)

SPREAD 5½ft (1.7m)

HABIT Tall, woody shrub

HARDINESS Z9–11 H12–9

FLOWERING Summer

A | 'Ariel'

THERE ARE TWO WAYS TO GROW 'ARIEL': either it can be left
alone to spread out its lax growth, or the growing tips can be
nipped out regularly in spring and early summer to encourage
it to bush out. Although on the small side, the multitude of
magenta and pink flowers creates a gentle, pretty effect; these
are followed by round, black berries. The tiny leaves, which
are dark green and glossy, are perfectly in proportion to the
flowers. Such daintiness makes it a perfect subject for bonsai,
although, if grown as a taller shrub, it would be a highlight in
a pastel border. It also tolerates full sun.

PLANT PROFILE

HEIGHT 2ft (60cm)

SPREAD 18in (45cm)

HABIT Lax bush, self-branching

HARDINESS Half hardy

FLOWERING Summer to first frost

'Army Nurse'

IN MILDER WINTERS THIS FUCHSIA will be able to take care of itself, but if severe frost is expected, a thick mulch of shredded bark over the crown wouldn't hurt. Although the semidouble flowers—deep carmine tube and sepals and bluish violet corolla—are on the small side, they reliably appear in large numbers. The plant makes a vigorous, bushy shape over summer and is highly recommended as the centerpiece in an ornamental tub, blending well with pastels or stronger, rich colors. It is an easy cultivar to grow.

PLANT PROFILE

HEIGHT 3–4ft (1–1.2m)

SPREAD 3ft (1m)

HABIT Upright bush

HARDINESS Frost hardy

FLOWERING Summer

A

'Aubergine'

A DARK EGGPLANT FUCHSIA is a nice change from more bright and brash colors. For maximum impact, plant it against a pale background, or grow it among a group of white and pink fuchsias for a marked contrast. 'Aubergine' is listed as a bush plant, but its stems are sufficiently lax and droopy that, with a little encouragement and judicious training, it will grow well in a hanging basket.

PLANT PROFILE		
HEIGHT 12–15in (30–38cm)		
SPREAD 18–24in (45–60cm)		
HABIT Bush, lax stems		
HARDINESS Half hardy		
FLOWERING Summer to first frost		

'Auntie Jinks'

A GOOD SHOW IS GUARANTEED with 'Auntie Jinks', which more than makes up for the fact that it is notoriously tricky to keep over winter. Just in case the parent does not survive, take autumn cuttings so you have a good supply of new plants for next summer. This is one of the best fuchsias for a hanging basket because it is short in stature, with lax, trailing stems. It is also very free-flowering, producing masses of small, single, white and pink-red blooms over a long period.

PLANT PROFILE	
HEIGHT 6–8in (15–20cm)	
SPREAD 8–16in (20–40cm)	
HABIT Trailing	
HARDINESS Z9–11 H12–9	
FLOWERING Summer to first frost	

A | 'Autumnale'

WORTH GROWING FOR TWO REASONS: first, 'Autumnale' is short and compact with stiff, horizontal branches that make it an ideal subject for hanging baskets; and second, the foliage adds extra interest before the single flowers appear in late summer. The emergent leaves are tinged with yellow and gradually take on dark red and salmon tints with a dash of yellow. Once you have seen the color change, its other name of 'Burning Bush' makes sense. Since this fuchsia is grown mainly for its foliage color, regular pinching out is recommended to ensure a ready supply of fresh leaves.

PLANT PROFILE

HEIGHT 6–12in (15–30cm)

SPREAD 12–24in (30–60cm)

HABIT Prostrate, horizontal bush

HARDINESS Z9–11 H12–9

FLOWERING Late summer to first frost

'Baby Bright'

THE DOMINANT COLOR IS WHITE but the whole flower, from the top of the tube to the tips of the winglike sepals, is flushed with pink. In a busy border, the small flowers of 'Baby Bright' are easily lost, so give it a solo spot in a small, ornamental pot—choose one made of terracotta and the warm-colored clay will enhance the pink tones of the petals. For the best effect, stand the pot against a dark background in dappled light; except at dawn and dusk when the light levels are low, bright sun bleaches out the gentle blush.

PLANT PROFILE

HEIGHT 6–9in (15–23cm)

SPREAD 6in (15cm)

HABIT Bush

HARDINESS Half hardy

FLOWERING Summer to first frost

B | x *bacillaris*

GIVEN WINTER PROTECTION, such as a thick mulch of
shredded bark, this small shrub will survive outdoors in the
border all year in many areas. It makes an attractive, upright or
spreading shape with thin, wiry stems bearing small, lance-
shaped leaves with hairy margins. The delicate pink to deep
red flowers are tiny—just ¼–⅜in (5–8mm) across—and appear
throughout summer and autumn. They are followed by shiny,
round, purple-brown fruit. The hybrid 'Cottinghamii' is similar
but makes a slightly larger bush.

PLANT PROFILE

HEIGHT 2–4ft (60–120cm)

SPREAD 2–4ft (60–120cm)

HABIT Erect or spreading

HARDINESS Z9–11 H12–9

FLOWERING Summer to autumn

'Ballerina Blue'

B

AN ELEGANT CULTIVAR with an upright habit that is useful in window boxes and as a center plant in hanging baskets. The small, pendent flowers are strongly colored, with bright red tube and sepals and deep blue corolla. They are produced in great numbers from early in the season right through to the first frost. The pistil and stamens are noticeably long and extend far below the hem of the corolla. This particular fuchsia is quite fussy about watering—don't let the soil dry out or it will drop its petals in protest.

PLANT PROFILE	
HEIGHT 8–10in (20–25cm)	
SPREAD 8–10in (20–25cm)	
HABIT Compact, upright bush	
HARDINESS Half hardy	
FLOWERING Early summer to first frost	

B | **'Ballet Girl'**

AN EXCELLENT BEGINNER'S FUCHSIA, this easy-going, vigorous cultivar was introduced back in 1894. Upright in habit, elegant, and full of poise, 'Ballet Girl' certainly lives up to its name. The large, showy, double flowers are an old favorite—the contrast between the cerise sepals and the frilly, tutulike white corolla is very eye-catching. This fuchsia deserves its place in the limelight and should be grown at the front of a bed or trained as a standard for planting in an ornamental pot.

PLANT PROFILE

HEIGHT	12–18in (30–45cm)
SPREAD	18–30in (45–75cm)
HABIT	Upright, bushy
HARDINESS	Z9–11 H12–9
FLOWERING	Summer to first frost

'Barbara'

B

A GENTLE-COLORED FUCHSIA, 'Barbara' is a blend of soft pinks.
But don't be fooled by the fey looks, which belie a strong,
vigorous nature—in summer this cultivar experiences a
growth spurt, throwing out new branches at an amazing rate.
A little on the unruly side, if tamed and trained it will make
a good standard or pillar. The light green leaves set off the
pastel-colored, single flowers to perfection. The only drawback
is a tendency to drop its flowers rather quickly but, as they are
produced in such profusion, there is little let-up in the display.
It copes well in full sun.

PLANT PROFILE

HEIGHT 24in (60cm)

SPREAD 24–30in (60–75cm)

HABIT Upright bush,
self-branching

HARDINESS Half hardy

FLOWERING Summer to first frost

B | 'Beacon'

THIS HIGHLY REGARDED, UNFUSSY FUCHSIA has stood the test of time—it was introduced in 1871 and still remains a popular choice for beginners. The dark green, wavy-edged leaves are the perfect foil for the brash, brightly colored flowers, which are a combination of deep pink tube and sepals and mauve-pink corolla. Compact bushiness and a pert, upright stance, together with an abundance of flowers, are the qualities that make it an outstanding bedding plant.

PLANT PROFILE	
HEIGHT 24in (60cm)	
SPREAD 24in (60cm)	
HABIT Compact, upright bush	
HARDINESS Z8–10	
FLOWERING Summer to autumn	

'Bealings'

B

A TOP-QUALITY PLANT that is worth growing if you want to pick up a prize at the local flower show. The flowers are striking without being strident, and are an eye-catching mix of waxy white and violet. Vigorous, upright, bushy growth makes it suitable for most forms of training. The perfect setting for 'Bealings' would be a solo spot in a pot on the garden table or, better still, raised on a plinth in the center of a small circular bed encircled by patio roses.

PLANT PROFILE

HEIGHT 9–12in (23–30cm)

SPREAD 6–9in (15–23cm)

HABIT Upright bush

HARDINESS Half hardy

FLOWERING Summer to first frost

B 'Beauty of Clyffe Hall'

THIS IS AN OLD FAVORITE from the Victorian grower James Lye. The smallish single flowers are a combination of pale dawn-pink, waxy tube and sepals teamed with a strong purple-red corolla. The red is echoed in the strong veining on the foliage. Inclined to be rather lax, it will need little encouragement to grow over a low wall or the edge of a raised bed. However, if given a good framework of supports and early pinching, it will also make a handsome bush. It is named after Clyffe Hall, where Lye worked as head gardener.

PLANT PROFILE	
HEIGHT 6–9in (15–23cm)	
SPREAD 18in (45cm)	
HABIT Lax bush	
HARDINESS Z8–10	
FLOWERING Summer to autumn	

'Bella Rosella'

B

LARGER-THAN-AVERAGE FLOWERS in an elegant blend of colors single this fuchsia out as something special. The tube and sepals are the palest pink with just a hint of greenish white, while the corolla is rich mauve with a hem of magenta. The heavy buds hang down from the stems like miniature Chinese lanterns. Since its introduction in North America in 1989, 'Bella Rosella' has wooed an increasing number of fans. The lax, trailing stems make it ideal for hanging baskets.

PLANT PROFILE

HEIGHT 6–9in (15–23cm)

SPREAD 18–24in (45–60cm)

HABIT Trailing

HARDINESS Half hardy

FLOWERING Summer to first frost

B | 'Ben Jammin'

A POPULAR CHOICE FOR ITS ABUNDANT SHOW of flowers in
a subtle mix of colors. If you want to grow something out
of the ordinary but find 'Aubergine' too somber, then 'Ben
Jammin' may be just what you're looking for. Its flowers are
a distinctive combination of soft pink tube, pinkish eggplant
sepals, and rich, dark eggplant corolla. Upright and compact, it
will make an attractive short-stemmed standard.

PLANT PROFILE

HEIGHT 24in (60cm)

SPREAD 12–15in (30–38cm)

HABIT Upright, compact bush,
self-branching

HARDINESS Half hardy

FLOWERING Summer to first frost

'Beverley'

THE BELL-LIKE, SINGLE FLOWERS of 'Beverley' have a daintiness about them that belies their generous proportions. They also appear in great profusion, which is unusual for a large-flowered fuchsia. 'Beverley' is suitable for all forms of upright training and will make a neat standard about 24in (60cm) tall. Plant it in a tub encircled by the wiry stems and bright yellow, daisylike flowers of *Bidens ferulifolia*. Alternatively, grow it as a bush for the front of the border with a backdrop of bush roses in a cottage-garden plan.

PLANT PROFILE

HEIGHT	24in (60cm)
SPREAD	12–18in (30–45cm)
HABIT	Upright bush
HARDINESS	Half hardy
FLOWERING	Summer to first frost

B | 'Beverly Hills'

A VERY GLAMOROUS FUCHSIA, with large double flowers that
appear in clusters. They are a beautiful coupling of pale pink
tube and upswept sepals with a heavily ruffled, blue corolla
that matures to lavender. If you make the effort to pinch out
the plant immediately after planting, it will quickly thicken up
to make a superb hanging basket plant.

PLANT PROFILE

HEIGHT	16–10in (5–25cm)
SPREAD	10in (25cm)
HABIT	Lax, trailing
HARDINESS	Frost hardy
FLOWERING	Summer

'Bicentennial'

B

THE BEST WAY TO GROW 'BICENTENNIAL' is in a hanging basket where you can glance up into the flowers. As if the slender white tube, Indian orange sepals, and double corolla weren't colorful enough, there's a vibrant splash of magenta right in the center. With free-flowering stems that grow horizontally outward before trailing, 'Bicentennial' makes a well-rounded shape in a basket and an exceptional 'weeping' standard. Full sun produces the best flower color.

PLANT PROFILE	
HEIGHT	12–18in (30–45cm)
SPREAD	18–24in (45–60cm)
HABIT	Semi-trailing, self-branching
HARDINESS	Z9–11 H12–9
FLOWERING	Summer to first frost

B | 'Billy Green'

SALMON PINK, SINGLE BLOOMS with unusually long tubes, up
to 2in (5cm), signal that 'Billy Green' belongs to the Triphylla
Group of fuchsias. The flowers, which have short sepals with
yellow tips, appear at each leaf axil (where the leaf joins the
stem) on sturdy stems. In pleasant contrast, the leaves are a light
olive green. Easy to grow and tolerant of most conditions, this
vigorous plant will reach a good size in its first year. You will
need to provide a little warmth to keep it going over winter.
If conditions are favorable, flowering is virtually nonstop.

PLANT PROFILE

HEIGHT	18–24in (45–60cm)
SPREAD	12–18in (30–45cm)
HABIT	Upright bush
HARDINESS	Half hardy
FLOWERING	Summer to first frost

'Black Prince' Black fuchsia

B

STRONGLY COLORED AND EYE-CATCHING, from a distance the dark purple corolla of 'Black Prince' could be mistaken for velvety black and, teamed with the crimson tube and sepals, the effect is very stylish. While mostly single, the occasional semidouble bloom appears. Very free-flowering, it makes a reliable, easy-to-grow, small, upright bush that needs little pinching out to keep it in shape. It is also a very good subject for bonsai. A sunny spot, even indoors, would suit it well, but do not overwater it. 'Black Prince' is also often listed under the name 'Gruss aus dem Bodethal'.

PLANT PROFILE

HEIGHT 12–18in (30–45cm)

SPREAD 9–12in (23–30cm)

HABIT Upright bush

HARDINESS Z8–10

FLOWERING Summer to first frost

B | 'Blueberry Fizz'

A SUPERLATIVE BASKET FUCHSIA with implausibly large, fully
double flowers that put on a spectacular show. The beautiful
crumpled, purple-blue corolla is crowned with white sepals
which, as they mature, curve upward and develop a pink
blush. Few would disagree that this has to be one of the most
pleasing fuchsia color combinations available. Early pinching
out will encourage the trailing stems to branch and make a
good shape for a basket.

PLANT PROFILE

HEIGHT 9–12in (23–30cm)

SPREAD 18in (45cm)

HABIT Trailing

HARDINESS Half hardy

FLOWERING Summer to first frost

'Blue Bush'

B

Over winter 'Blue Bush' is all bare twigs and stems—some of which, despite its 'hardy' tag, will die back after a hard frost. Come spring, after pruning back to just above the lowest buds, vigorous new growth will quickly shoot up to waist height. If the bush looks spindly, keep pinching out the tips in spring and early summer to thicken it up. The flowers are a strong mix of pinkish red and violet-blue and are produced over a very long period. To help it survive a cold winter, cover the crown with a layer of shredded bark. 'Blue Bush' makes a wonderful flowering hedge.

PLANT PROFILE

HEIGHT 3–4ft (90–120cm)

SPREAD 3–4ft (90–120cm)

HABIT Upright bush

HARDINESS Fully hardy

FLOWERING Summer

B ## 'Blue Gown'

A LIVELY MIX OF COLORS gives this very old cultivar an outstanding presence in the border, where it will bring much-needed height to plantings of mixed annuals. Double flowers carry a cerise tube and sepals and a purplish blue corolla with pink and scarlet markings. The weight of the blooms makes staking essential. 'Blue Gown' is a good choice for large, early season flowers, while its strong, upright growth makes it an ideal subject for training as a standard.

PLANT PROFILE

HEIGHT 30–36in (75–90cm)

SPREAD 30–36in (75–90cm)

HABIT Upright bush

HARDINESS Half hardy

FLOWERING Early summer to first frost

'Blue Mirage'

B

EYE-CATCHING COLORS SET AGAINST A BACKDROP of dark green leaves, the large double flowers of 'Blue Mirage' are a mix of white tube and sepals, flushed with pink, and a corolla in a blend of pink and blue. Although the growth habit is described as trailing, it is actually fairly upright and very vigorous, making it suitable for hanging pots or baskets. While some of the stems shoot out horizontally, others grow straight up, giving the plant a spiky outline.

PLANT PROFILE

HEIGHT 6–12in (15–30cm)

SPREAD 12–18in (30–45cm)

HABIT Trailing, self-branching

HARDINESS Half hardy

FLOWERING Summer to first frost

B | *boliviana*

VIGOROUS AND BUSHY, this species fuchsia was introduced from Bolivia in 1876. Listed as a small tree or shrub, it has arching growth with large, dark green, red-veined leaves that are 8in (20cm) long and covered in downy hairs. It produces tight, drooping clusters of 2in- (5cm-) long, slender flowers all summer, followed by purple berries. It is best grown in a large pot—its roots must not be cramped—in a conservatory against a warm, sunny wall. The branches are a strong red when young, aging to brown and developing peeling bark. For red and white flowers, grow *F. boliviana* var. *alba*.

PLANT PROFILE	
HEIGHT 12ft (4m)	
SPREAD 3–4ft (1–1.2m)	
HABIT Shrub, small tree, or climber	
HARDINESS Z13–15 H12–9	
FLOWERING Summer to autumn	

boliviana var. *alba*

B

VERY SIMILAR IN HABIT AND FORM to *F. boliviana*, except that the flowers of this species fuchsia have white sepals and tube, while the stems and berries are light green. Again, although it is listed as a shrub or small tree, it is happiest growing against a warm, sunny wall in a conservatory. It will eventually make a sizeable plant, so give it a good-sized pot.

PLANT PROFILE	
HEIGHT 12ft (4m)	
SPREAD 3–4ft (1–1.2m)	
HABIT Shrub, small tree, or climber	
HARDINESS Z13–15 H12–9	
FLOWERING Summer to autumn	

B

'Bon Accorde'

THE STEMS OF THIS CULTIVAR are sturdy enough to hold the small, single, ivory and pale lilac flowers nicely erect above the mid-green foliage. Produced in great abundance, the blooms make a real impression. Although growth is naturally bushy and upright, give the plant a helping hand by pinching out the growing tips in the early stages. Use a few at the front of a border or train it as a small standard.

PLANT PROFILE

HEIGHT 18–24in (45–60cm)

SPREAD 12–18in (30–45cm)

HABIT Upright bush

HARDINESS Z9–11 H12–9

FLOWERING Summer to first frost

'Bordeaux Belle'

B

A NEW FUCHSIA FOR THE 21ST CENTURY, 'Bordeaux Belle' is a fashionably subtle mix of eggplant tones, with the tube a paler shade than the sepals and corolla. It will keep its color better in light shade than full sun. Growth is small, bushy, and just right for an ornamental pot on a patio or garden dining table. Alternatively, use a few plants to edge a summer border.

PLANT PROFILE

HEIGHT 12in (30cm)

SPREAD 12in (30cm)

HABIT Compact bush

HARDINESS Half hardy

FLOWERING Summer to first frost

B | 'Border Queen'

A CLASSY PINK FUCHSIA with bell-shaped flowers that are well presented on quick-growing, upright, branching stems. The amethyst-violet corolla carries particularly striking markings—the neatly furled petals are flushed with pale pink and bear dark pink veining. 'Border Queen' is ideal as a focal point among other shorter fuchsias, or use it to fill gaps among young shrubs that have yet to fill out.

PLANT PROFILE
HEIGHT 18–24in (45–60cm)
SPREAD 18in (45cm)
HABIT Upright bush self-branching
HARDINESS Half hardy
FLOWERING Summer to first frost

'Börnemann's Beste'

B

IF YOU WANT SOMETHING DIFFERENT, try this unusual-looking Triphylla fuchsia with its clusters of elegant, long, slender, vibrant orange-red flowers. A lively addition to a cottage garden, it is also at home in a hothouse or subtropical planting growing beside brightly colored cannas or dahlias and large-leaved plants, such as daturas. Strong-growing and very vigorous, when planted among small ornamental grasses, it makes a bright, punchy impact and perfectly balances their airy sprays of midsummer flowers.

PLANT PROFILE
HEIGHT 18–24in (45–60cm)
SPREAD 12–18in (30–45cm)
HABIT Bush
HARDINESS Frost tender
FLOWERING Summer

B | 'Bow Bells'

LARGE, ELEGANT, SINGLE FLOWERS appear relatively early in the summer; by the end of the season they are produced in such numbers that they start to weigh down the stems, giving the plant a weeping habit. Support may be necessary to stop stems from snapping. This is a useful fuchsia for full or partial shade, where its magenta and white flowers will brighten the gloom. A bush with a spreading habit, it would be suitable for a large container, or train it as a standard.

PLANT PROFILE

HEIGHT 18–24in (45–60cm)

SPREAD 24in (60cm)

HABIT Spreading bush

HARDINESS Half hardy

FLOWERING Summer to first frost

'Brighton Belle'

B

A SOFTLY COLORED, NON–SHOWY FUCHSIA with clusters of
dangling, long, thin, rose red and salmon pink flowers (it is a
Triphylla) that show up well against the dark green foliage.
The growth habit is spreading and full, which makes it a good
choice for a hanging basket. 'Brighton Belle' can also be
grown at the front of a border, where it will spread on to the
path, injecting an easy-going, cottage-garden feel.

PLANT PROFILE	
HEIGHT 18–24in (45–60cm)	
SPREAD 12–18in (30–45cm)	
HABIT Bush, self-branching	
HARDINESS Frost tender	
FLOWERING Summer	

B | 'Brilliant'

BRIGHT AND BRASH, this fuchsia puts on a neat display of scarlet and violet-magenta single flowers and is a perfect partner for small ornamental grasses in the hardy border. With a covering of shredded bark, 'Brilliant' is sufficiently tough to withstand winter outdoors in cool-climate gardens. Training is vital to achieve a neatly shaped bush, so start pinching out the growing tips while stems are still young or you will end up with a sprawling plant.

PLANT PROFILE
HEIGHT 24–30in (60–75cm)
SPREAD 18–24in (45–60cm)
HABIT Upright, bushy
HARDINESS Fully hardy
FLOWERING Summer

'Brutus'

B

TRUSTY, RELIABLE, AND VERSATILE—what more could a gardener ask for? First introduced over 100 years ago, 'Brutus' has stood the test of time and remains justly popular today. Even if conditions are less than perfect, it will still put on a good show. It produces an abundance of flowers (cerise tube and sepals and dark purple corollas that age to reddish purple) early in the season. Upright, vigorous, and bushy, it looks good in the border or in a container, and is also easily trained as a standard or pillar. In warm areas, it can be used as an informal hedge.

PLANT PROFILE

HEIGHT 24in (60cm)

SPREAD 24in (60cm)

HABIT Upright bush

HARDINESS Z9–11 H12–9

FLOWERING Summer to autumn

C | 'Cambridge Louie'

AN EXQUISITE SHADE OF PINKISH ORANGE ensures that the blooms of 'Cambridge Louie' always catch the eye. Appearing with tireless frequency over summer, the flowers are of such beauty that they deserve a prominent place in an ornamental container. Highlight them against a dark background for the best effect. Pinching out the growing tips in spring and early summer will improve the bushiness of the plant.

PLANT PROFILE

HEIGHT 18–24in (45–60cm)

SPREAD 18–24in (45–60cm)

HABIT Upright bush, self-branching

HARDINESS Half hardy

FLOWERING Summer to first frost

'Cardinal Farges'

C

BRIGHT RED AND WHITE FLOWERS cover the branches of this
vigorous cultivar, and look from a distance like dozens of
mini–Santa Clauses dancing among the mid-green leaves. Bold
enough to be the centerpiece in almost any display, the one
problem with this jolly plant is that its woody stems tend to
be brittle. Plant it where it will be sheltered from buffeting
winds and provide a good framework of canes for support.

PLANT PROFILE	
HEIGHT 15–18in (38–45cm)	
SPREAD 12–15in (30–38cm)	
HABIT Upright bush, self-branching	
HARDINESS Frost hardy	
FLOWERING Summer	

C | 'Carla Johnston'

THE DELICATE-COLORED, BELL-SHAPED FLOWERS of 'Carla Johnston' are a subtle combination of pale sea lavender and baby pink with an undertone of spring green. Raised in the UK in 1986, this free-flowering, upright fuchsia makes an excellent standard or neatly shaped bush. Its understated, modern look is best appreciated at the front of a summer border or in an ornamental patio planter.

PLANT PROFILE

HEIGHT 18–24in (45–60cm)

SPREAD 18–24in (45–60cm)

HABIT Upright bush, self-branching

HARDINESS Half hardy

FLOWERING Summer to first frost

'Carmel Blue'

ONE OF THE BEST BLUE AND WHITE CULTIVARS, 'Carmel Blue' has exceptional flowers that are freely produced over summer. The tubes and long, graceful sepals are almost pure white (with just a hint of green on the former and pink on the latter), while the corolla is a lovely blue, aging to soft purple. Protect the color of the petals by growing it in dappled shade. This stunning fuchsia has star quality and shouldn't languish at the back of the border; give it a lead role in your plantings, or plant a pair in ornate pots and use them to mark the entrance to your home or yard.

PLANT PROFILE

HEIGHT 12–18in (30–45cm)

SPREAD 12–15in (30–38cm)

HABIT Upright bush, self-branching

HARDINESS Z10

FLOWERING Summer to first frost

C | 'Cascade'

THE NAMING OF SOME PLANTS is often a puzzle, but it is easy
to see why 'Cascade' is so called. It is a perfect fuchsia for a
hanging basket, where its trailing stems will tumble freely over
the sides. To add to the effect, a profusion of single white and
carmine flowers hang from the very tips of the branches.
When trained as a standard, the stems will adopt an attractive
weeping habit. The only minor drawback to this lovely fuchsia
is the lack of flowers on its topgrowth.

PLANT PROFILE

HEIGHT 6–12in (15–30cm)

SPREAD 12–18in (30–45cm)

HABIT Trailing, self-branching

HARDINESS Z9–11 H12–9

FLOWERING Summer to first frost

'Casper Hauser'

A MASS OF DEEP RED, DOUBLE FLOWERS and bushy, dark green foliage makes 'Casper Hauser' a very striking fuchsia. A lovely, upright plant for the summer border, it makes an especially effective color link with slightly paler fuchsias in a group display. Grow it in pots to brighten up a patio, conservatory, or greenhouse. Considering that its rich tones combine so well with summer bedding, it is surprising that 'Casper Hauser' isn't more widely grown.

C

PLANT PROFILE

HEIGHT 18–24in (45–60cm)

SPREAD 18–24in (45–60cm)

HABIT Upright bush, self-branching

HARDINESS Half hardy

FLOWERING Summer to first frost

C | 'Celia Smedley'

STAR BILLING IS WELL DESERVED for 'Celia Smedley', and it's a popular choice for both gardeners and expert growers alike. It delivers the goods, making a strong impact even in its first summer, and produces a mass of exquisite, larger-than-average flowers, with currant red corollas and dark pink, upswept sepals. The leaves are large, shapely, and a rich mid-green. As you'd expect from a plant that gets off to such a good start, growth is vigorous, and its strong, vertical stems make it a natural choice for training as a standard. It is also excellent as a bedder or in containers. Regular pinching out is essential.

PLANT PROFILE

HEIGHT 18–30in (45–75cm)

SPREAD 18–30in (45–75cm)

HABIT Upright bush, self-branching

HARDINESS Z9–11 H12–9

FLOWERING Summer to first frost

'Chang'

C

'CHANG' IS AN EXTROVERT that demands attention. The profuse, single flowers are a bright, brash orange, with just a hint of red in the tube. The plant shoots away, so if you intend to grow it in a pot, make sure it's substantial enough to stabilize the exuberant topgrowth, or a strong wind will send it flying. Alternatively, nip out the growing tips regularly to increase bushiness and keep the plant more compact. For the best show of flowers, grow 'Chang' outdoors. This cultivar is susceptible to botrytis and as a result should not be overwatered.

PLANT PROFILE	
HEIGHT	24–30in (60–75cm)
SPREAD	24–30in (60–75cm)
HABIT	Upright bush
HARDINESS	Z8–10
FLOWERING	Summer to first frost

C | 'Charlie Dimmock'

BUSHY AND BLOWZY, this cultivar makes a decent-sized plant with strong, vigorous growth. The flowers have dullish, dark red sepals and tubes, with frilly purple corollas. Nip out the growing tips in spring and early summer to create a nice, rounded shape. A good choice for containers and summer borders; ensure that the colors stand out by planting it in front of a light background—a small, ornamental grass would be an ideal planting companion.

PLANT PROFILE		
HEIGHT 15–18in (38–45cm)		
SPREAD 12–15in (30–38cm)		
HABIT Upright bush		
HARDINESS Half hardy		
FLOWERING Summer to first frost		

'Charming'

FULL OF CHARM, AS ITS NAME SUGGESTS, the single flowers—carmine tube, upswept reddish purple sepals, and rosy purple corolla—contrast well with the foliage, which is predominantly yellowish green. Toward the leaf tips, the color drains away, becoming very pale. This strong-growing, upright bush will quickly become a mass of tightly packed, strong stems, but the overall impression is one of shapeliness rather than sprawl. An easy fuchsia to grow, this is a good starter plant for beginners.

C

PLANT PROFILE

HEIGHT 18–30in (45–75cm)

SPREAD 24–30in (60–75cm)

HABIT Upright bush

HARDINESS Frost hardy

FLOWERING Summer

C | 'Checkerboard'

ALWAYS EYE-CATCHING, 'Checkerboard' has been popular since its introduction in 1948. Easy to grow, it is a beautiful, upright fuchsia for bedding or training as a standard, with stiff but not thick stems. It is not suitable for a basket. Elegant flowers are produced very early and in great abundance, and although they don't last long on the bush before dropping, they are quickly replaced. The markings are interesting too: the rich red color on the tube bleeds into the white sepals and is picked up again on the corolla, but in a deeper tone.

PLANT PROFILE

HEIGHT 30–36in (75–90cm)

SPREAD 18–30in (45–75cm)

HABIT Upright bush

HARDINESS Z9–11 H12–9

FLOWERING Early summer to first frost

'Chillerton Beauty'

C

FASHIONABLY FADED IS HOW TO DESCRIBE the small, single flowers of this fuchsia as they age—the faintly veined corolla slowly lightens from blue to a soft purple-magenta. Growth is upright, vigorous, and arching, with an excellent show of flowers. In milder areas it is hardy enough to be left in the border all year to make an attractive, informal hedge. Easy to grow, it performs best in a sunny position.

PLANT PROFILE

HEIGHT 30–36in (75–90cm)

SPREAD 30–36in (75–90cm)

HABIT Upright, arching

HARDINESS Frost hardy

FLOWERING Summer

C

'Circus Spangles'

PREPARE TO BE DAZZLED by this 1990 North American introduction, which is a lively combination of bright white tube and sepals and a white-flecked red corolla. The flowers are fully double and produced in great numbers, making it a real show-stopper. It has lax, trailing stems and a very vigorous growth habit, so that even in its first year, it will easily fill out a hanging basket or planter.

PLANT PROFILE

HEIGHT 12–15in (30–38cm)

SPREAD 18–24in (45–60cm)

HABIT Trailing

HARDINESS Half hardy

FLOWERING Summer to first frost

'Clipper'

C

GET THE SUMMER OFF TO A GOOD START with this early
flowering, vigorous fuchsia. The single blooms, which appear
nonstop throughout summer, have a purple corolla that ages to
a rich claret red. The combination of lush, mid-green foliage on
strong red stems is also very striking. If you can find one or,
better still, two ready-trained as standards, use them to mark
the entrance to the garden, the start of a pathway, or potted up
in an ornamental container as the focal point in an island bed.

PLANT PROFILE

HEIGHT 18in (45cm)

SPREAD 18–24in (45–60cm)

HABIT Upright bush

HARDINESS Half hardy

FLOWERING Summer to first frost

C

'Cloth of Gold'

GROWN FOR ITS STUNNING FOLIAGE, the gold in this fuchsia refers to the burnished yellow leaves that age to a copper-green with red on the reverse. As on many foliage plants, the flowers are late to open and, when they do, are not freely produced. Single and of medium size, the blooms have a red tube and sepals and a purple corolla. Positioning 'Cloth of Gold' beside a fuchsia with dark leaves will bring out the foliage contrast; ideally, if its planting partner also has white or pink blooms, the red flowers will be highlighted, too.

PLANT PROFILE

HEIGHT 12–15in (30–38cm)

SPREAD 10–12in (25–30cm)

HABIT Upright bush

HARDINESS Half hardy

FLOWERING Summer to first frost

'Coachman'

C

YOUR ARE IN LUCK if you find a nursery that sells 'Coachman' trained as a standard. Planted in a big pot, this early-flowering fuchsia in a rich mix of salmon and orange will create a warm welcome by the front door. An easy cultivar to train, you will usually find it for sale as summer bedding or a hanging basket plant. Pinch out new stems in spring and early summer and you will be rewarded with ever-stronger flushes of flowers on the vigorous, bushy growth. You will also boost the supply of large, rich green leaves.

PLANT PROFILE

HEIGHT	18–24in (45–60cm)
SPREAD	18–24in (45–60cm)
HABIT	Lax bush
HARDINESS	Half hardy
FLOWERING	Summer to first frost

C | 'Comet'

A FUCHSIA WITH PLENTY OF PLUSES that is well deserving of its dramatic name, 'Comet' tends to get off to an early flowering start, way ahead of many others, and then keeps going throughout the summer. The large, single blooms are produced on strong, upright growth and consist of a red tube and sepals with violet-blue corolla. The blue tones provide a good contrast among groupings of red and white or red and pink fuchsias. To really appreciate the richness of the petal color, try planting 'Comet' in a pot or border set against a light background.

PLANT PROFILE

HEIGHT 12–18in (30–45cm)

SPREAD 9–12in (23–30cm)

HABIT Upright bush, self-branching

HARDINESS Half hardy

FLOWERING Summer to first frost

'Constance'

THIS FUCHSIA IS A GOOD MIXER. A blend of pretty pinks, 'Constance' would make a good bedfellow with other hardy fuchsias that have strong, red-toned flowers. Allow their stems to intertwine and you will create an attractive, two-tone bush. A perfect plant for the cottage garden, grow it in front of leggy roses to hide their bare stems, or use it to soften the edge of a pond. It is a very free-flowering, upright plant that is hardy enough to be left out all year in mild areas. It can also be trained to any shape, but isn't suitable for a hanging basket.

PLANT PROFILE	
HEIGHT	12–18in (30–45cm)
SPREAD	12–18in (30–45cm)
HABIT	Upright bush
HARDINESS	Borderline hardy
FLOWERING	Summer to first frost

C | 'Coralle'

THE LONG, SLENDER TUBES of this fuchsia mark it out as
coming from the Triphylla Group. The slender orange flowers,
which have neatly cut, salmon pink sepals, appear in tight,
pendent clusters at the very tips of the strong, upright stems.
The longish leaves are olive green with a velvety covering of
fine hairs. Trained as a standard and grown in a pot, 'Coralle'
would make a stunning feature plant for a cool conservatory
or sheltered patio. Avoid strong midday sun, which could cause
the plant to wilt. Although not as frost-shy as most Triphylla
fuchsias, play it safe and bring it under cover in a cold snap.

PLANT PROFILE

HEIGHT 18–36in (45–90cm)

SPREAD 18–24in (45–60cm)

HABIT Upright

HARDINESS Z13–15 H12–9

FLOWERING Summer to autumn

'Corallina'

C

WITH SO MANY PLUS POINTS, it is hard to know where to begin. For starters, this fuchsia makes a dense, bushy plant that is packed with flowers over a long season. Its blooms are a rich blend of scarlet, purple, and pink, while the dark green foliage has the added dimension of a bronze tint. A vigorous spreader with branches that are more horizontal than trailing, it would make a pretty, informal hedge. The slightly smaller 'Corallina Variegata' has the same flower color but its early foliage is red, turning a variegated mix of cream, green, and cerise. One point to remember: young plants hate being overwatered.

PLANT PROFILE	
HEIGHT	36in (90cm)
SPREAD	36–48in (90–120cm)
HABIT	Spreading bush
HARDINESS	Frost hardy
FLOWERING	Summer to autumn

C | *cordifolia*

INTRIGUING AND EXCEPTIONAL, *F. cordifolia* is grown for its slender, tubelike flowers, which appear in each leaf axil (where the leaf joins the stem). Introduced in the mid-19th century from Guatemala, some experts now consider it to be a hybrid of *F. splendens*. Whatever its genealogy, its simple charms make it a welcome change from fancier fuchsias, and it is worth growing in the summer border as a feature plant, or in a large container for the conservatory.

PLANT PROFILE	
HEIGHT	18in (45cm)
SPREAD	18in (45cm)
HABIT	Lax bush
HARDINESS	Frost tender
FLOWERING	Summer

'Countess of Aberdeen'

ONE OF THE FINEST NEAR-WHITE FUCHSIAS, the graceful 'Countess' is an outstanding plant. Even if you don't have a special position for it, buy one knowing that it is an invaluable gap-filler. For the best effect, grow it in front of dark evergreen shrubs or in a pot beside a red-brick wall. You could also use it to cool down bright plantings of reds and blues, or to extend a range of pastels. In full sun the pink undertone in the petals becomes stronger, and to retain its pallor you need to grow it in dappled shade. Avoid overwatering too, since this makes plants prone to botrytis.

PLANT PROFILE	
HEIGHT	18–24in (45–60cm)
SPREAD	15–18in (38–45cm)
HABIT Upright bush, self-branching	
HARDINESS	Half hardy
FLOWERING	Summer to first frost

D | 'Daisy Bell'

A GOOD CHOICE FOR A HANGING BASKET, the stems of 'Daisy Bell' are naturally trailing, vigorous, and self-branching. Although the flowers are small, they are produced in huge numbers, and the petal color is a vibrant combination of white and citrus orange. Orange is a very useful color in baskets, helping to jazz up arrangements that may be a touch too timid. The olive green leaves are pale underneath with red veining—a secret that is only revealed if the basket is hung high enough. Grow this cultivar in full sun for the best leaf and flower color.

PLANT PROFILE	
HEIGHT 9–12in (23–30cm)	
SPREAD 18–24in (45–60cm)	
HABIT Trailing, self-branching	
HARDINESS Half hardy	
FLOWERING Summer to first frost	

'Dancing Flame'

D

THE ALL-ORANGE FLOWERS (with darker stripes on the tube and a deeper shade on the corolla) have plenty of zing, despite their diminutive size. Depending on the shade, orange can sometimes be a tricky color to handle, but if you remember to give it a dark background, you won't go far wrong. 'Dancing Flame' has naturally trailing stems, but they are rather stiff and will need tweaking to get them to fill a hanging basket—attaching light weights will do the trick. If you prefer to grow it as a bush, use supports to keep it looking neat.

PLANT PROFILE

HEIGHT 12–15in (30–38cm)

SPREAD 15–18in (38–45cm)

HABIT Trailing

HARDINESS Half hardy

FLOWERING Summer to first frost

D | **'Dark Eyes'**

A PRIZE-WINNING AMERICAN FUCHSIA, with strong, bushy growth and plenty of medium-sized, rich-colored, double flowers. First introduced in 1958, 'Dark Eyes' still has cachet. The name refers to the contrast between the red tube and sepals and the deep violet-blue corolla. While many other fuchsia blooms are full and frilly, this one retains a neat, tight form. It makes an exceptional standard and, as a focal point in a border or container, it is hard to beat. It is only a summer resident in the garden and must be brought under cover for the winter.

PLANT PROFILE

HEIGHT 18–24in (45–60cm)

SPREAD 24–30in (60–75cm)

HABIT Upright bush, self-branching

HARDINESS Z9–11 H12–9

FLOWERING Summer to first frost

'David'

D

JUSTIFIABLY POPULAR, WITH A PROLIFIC SHOW of cerise and rich purple flowers, 'David' is a short-growing, compact fuchsia. However, it is easily lost among taller plants, and is best used at the front of a display as a low, bushy hedge. It is particularly effective where the plants behind it are either white or red—shrub roses would be a good match. Used in a subtropical plan, it looks stunning when contrasted with the large, copper-colored leaves of the castor bean (*Ricinus communis*).

PLANT PROFILE

HEIGHT	15–18in (38–45cm)
SPREAD	18–24in (45–60cm)
HABIT	Low-growing bush
HARDINESS	Z8–10
FLOWERING	Summer

D | 'Dawn Star'

TYPICAL OF RECENT INTRODUCTIONS, this cultivar has an abundance of large, double flowers that are produced on vigorous, upright stems. The blooms are a jazzy combination of red tube and sepals and a violet corolla, and the foliage is a good strong green. Despite their sturdiness, the stems often appear weighed down by the heavy blooms, but they won't break. Although the plant is naturally bushy, diligent pinching out of the growing tips will plump it up even more.

PLANT PROFILE

HEIGHT 15–18in (38–45cm)

SPREAD 12–18in (30–45cm)

HABIT Strong, upright bush

HARDINESS Half hardy

FLOWERING Summer to first frost

'Deep Purple'

D

LARGE, FRILLY, DOUBLE FLOWERS, which are bright white and showy purple, look amazing when they tumble over the edges of a hanging basket. The lax, trailing stems are packed with buds and flowers all summer long. If trained as a standard, the stems of 'Deep Purple' will quickly form a distinctive mushroom-shaped top. Grow it in a large container that can be safely overwintered under cover.

PLANT PROFILE

HEIGHT 9–12in (23–30cm)

SPREAD 12–18in (30–45cm)

HABIT Trailing

HARDINESS Half hardy

FLOWERING Summer to first frost

D | 'Delta's Wonder'

WHEN FLOWERS ARE THIS LARGE it is unusual for them to be produced in such numbers, but 'Delta's Wonder' more than lives up to its name, putting on an exceptional show of striking, reddish purple and lilac purple blooms. The striping on the corolla is particularly attractive. Plant this fuchsia in the center of a large pot and surround it with white or pastel annuals so that its dark-colored blooms really stand out. Growth is fairly lax, so it will need staking on exposed sites.

PLANT PROFILE

HEIGHT 18in (45cm)

SPREAD 24–36in (60–90cm)

HABIT Upright bush

HARDINESS Half hardy

FLOWERING Summer to first frost

denticulata

D

A SPECIES FUCHSIA from Peru and Bolivia, *F. denticulata* has a quiet, gentle beauty. The slender, dangling flowers are a rare combination of light red, orange, pink, white, and green. They appear in each leaf axil (where the leaf joins the stem) and are more abundant in spring and autumn than summer. As the stems age, they change from green to wine red and develop tan-colored peeling bark. This easy-to-grow fuchsia is tolerant of sun and will put on a good show in the border; it also grows well in a pot in the conservatory. Despite being vigorous and upright, it can appear rather spindly.

PLANT PROFILE
HEIGHT 15–18in (38–45cm)
SPREAD 12–15in (30–38cm)
HABIT Upright, spindly bush
HARDINESS Z9–11 H12–9
FLOWERING Late spring to autumn

D | 'Devonshire Dumpling'

THE FAT, ROUND FLOWER BUDS of this fuchsia will make your
fingers itch to pop them. Buds open to large, double blooms
that have green-tipped, rose-colored sepals and a white corolla
flushed pink on the outer surface. Once this fuchsia starts
flowering, it just keeps going. Strong growth makes it suitable
for planting in a border or for training as a standard, but it really
excels when grown in a hanging basket. Do not overwater
your plants, since this will promote botrytis.

PLANT PROFILE

HEIGHT 12–15in (30–38cm)

SPREAD 18–24in (45–60cm)

HABIT Trailing

HARDINESS Half hardy

FLOWERING Summer to first frost

'Display'

RELIABLE AND EASY TO GROW, 'Display' produces a plethora of flowers on its vigorous, upright growth. One of the first fuchsias to flower, it continues unabated right through to the end of the season. Although naturally bushy, it can be encouraged to thicken up even more by nipping out the growing tips a couple of times. It grows well under many conditions, and can be trained to any shape. A good, strong root system means that it will survive outside all year in milder climates. As long as it has plenty of light and the atmosphere isn't too dry, it will also grow happily indoors.

D

PLANT PROFILE

HEIGHT 24–30in (60–75cm)

SPREAD 18–24in (45–60cm)

HABIT Upright bush

HARDINESS Z9–11 H12–9

FLOWERING Early summer to first frost

D | 'Doc'

THE CLASSIC FUCHSIA MIX of bright red tube and sepals with mauve corolla ensures that the flowers stand out well against the deep green leaves. In mild, frost-free areas, 'Doc' can be treated as an all-year garden plant, especially if a mulch of shredded bark is piled over the crown in winter, but in most areas it is best grown in a pot or dug up and brought under cover for winter. Its dwarf habit makes it ideal for the front of a hardy border. The flowers, which are freely produced, will stand out well against anything light, such as annuals with white flowers, silver leaves, or a whitewashed wall.

PLANT PROFILE

HEIGHT 9–15in (23–38cm)

SPREAD 9–12in (23–30cm)

HABIT Upright, dwarf bush

HARDINESS Borderline hardy

FLOWERING Summer

'Doctor Foster'

D

OFTEN LISTED AS 'DR. FOSTER', this is one of the largest flowering hardy fuchsias available. The rich green leaves are the perfect foil for the scarlet blooms, which have a hint of lilac in the corolla. With a thick mulch of shredded bark spread over the crown, it is hardy enough to survive outdoors in some regions. In warm areas it makes an attractive hedge. An elegant combination would be to plant 'Doctor Foster' among a bed of scented white lilies. Keep plants looking neat and encourage fresh, new growth to sprout by cutting stems back in spring to the lowest shoot.

PLANT PROFILE	
HEIGHT	36in (90cm)
SPREAD	36in (90cm)
HABIT	Upright bush
HARDINESS	Fully hardy
FLOWERING	Summer

D | 'Dollar Princess'

ALSO KNOWN AS 'PRINCESS DOLLAR', this very early flowering cultivar produces blooms that may be considered rather on the small side for doubles; however, what they lack in stature, they more than make up for in shapeliness and sheer numbers. It is an easy plant to grow and to train—growth is strong, fast, and very upright, and it makes a beautiful standard. Try using it in the border or as the central focus in a large pot of mixed plants.

PLANT PROFILE

HEIGHT 12–18in (30–45cm)

SPREAD 18–24in (45–60cm)

HABIT Upright bush, self-branching

HARDINESS Z9–11 H12–9

FLOWERING Summer to autumn

'Dopey'

D

ONE OF THE SMALLEST FUCHSIAS, 'Dopey' makes a dainty
feature plant for a small container. It produces a continuous
display of small, double flowers in a lively mix of red (on
the tube and sepals) and pink-purple (the corolla). This little
plant is all too easily overlooked in the busy aisles of the
garden center, which is a shame, considering its color mix
packs such a powerful punch. In mild areas it can be planted
in the border where it will survive winter outdoors, provided
the crown is covered with a thick layer of shredded bark.

PLANT PROFILE

HEIGHT 9–16in (23–40cm)

SPREAD 9–16in (23–40cm)

HABIT Upright, dwarf bush

HARDINESS Borderline hardy

FLOWERING Summer

D | 'Drame'

A VIRTUALLY ALL-RED, HARDY FUCHSIA, 'Drame' has flashy, bright red sepals and tube with the barest hint of mauve on the corolla. When young, the foliage is yellowish green, darkening to green with age. Together with dahlias, 'Drame' will inject life into the late summer border. A good, strong plant with upright, bushy, spreading growth, it would make an attractive flowering hedge. It is hardy enough to be left outside all year in many areas, provided the crown is covered with a layer of shredded bark.

PLANT PROFILE

HEIGHT 18–24in (45–60cm)

SPREAD 18–24in (45–60cm)

HABIT Upright bush, self-branching

HARDINESS Fully hardy

FLOWERING Summer

'Dusky Rose'

THE LONG, TRAILING STEMS of this cultivar will soon fill a hanging basket or wall-mounted pot with dark green foliage and large, ruffled, double flowers in wonderful shades of pink. As they mature, the colors subtly change—the rose red corolla fades to a delicate raspberry sherbet color. These blushing tones go well with a dark blue glazed pot, together with ivy-leaved pelargoniums in an equally soft shade of pink or cream, and trailing ivy. 'Dusky Rose' is noted for its heat tolerance and resistance to wilting.

PLANT PROFILE
HEIGHT 6–9in (15–23cm)
SPREAD 18–24in (45–60cm)
HABIT Trailing, self-branching
HARDINESS Half hardy
FLOWERING Summer to first frost

E | 'Eden Lady'

HYACINTH BLUE AND PALE ROSE—very 1970s (which was when this fuchsia was introduced) and now back in fashion. An easy-to-grow, general-purpose cultivar, it has short, bushy stems that keep it looking neat and tidy. If you pinch out the stems in spring and early summer, you can force extra growth from the base, encouraging it to thicken up even more and to boost flowering. For the best petal color, grow 'Eden Lady' in the shade.

PLANT PROFILE

HEIGHT 18–24in (45–60cm)

SPREAD 15–18in (38–45cm)

HABIT Upright bush, self-branching

HARDINESS Half hardy

FLOWERING Summer to first frost

'Elfin Glade'

E

PLENTY OF VIGOROUS, BUSHY GROWTH and a free-flowering habit make 'Elfin Glade' a good choice for containers and bedding. Although hardy enough to be left outside over winter in mild areas, it is better to be safe than sorry and cover plants with a thick mulch of shredded bark to protect them from severe frost. The two-tone flowers, with their reddish pink caps and rose-purple corolla, have a winsome charm that matches the name.

PLANT PROFILE	
HEIGHT 15in (38cm)	
SPREAD 18in (45cm)	
HABIT Upright bush	
HARDINESS Borderline frost hardy	
FLOWERING Summer	

E

'Elfriede Ott'

THE TELLTALE, LONG SLENDER TUBES of this fuchsia mark it out as being a member of the Triphylla Group. The very small salmon pink flowers have gently flared sepals that open to reveal a rose pink, curly-edged corolla. The flowers are borne in clusters and are set off by mid-green leaves with red veining. It is a good choice for bedding displays and hanging baskets, but for the best show, it must have a warm, sheltered spot with plenty of sunshine. If grown indoors in good light and kept at a temperature of around 60°F (15°C), it should keep flowering over winter.

PLANT PROFILE

HEIGHT	18–24in (45–60cm)
SPREAD	12–18in (30–45cm)
HABIT	Lax upright or stiff trailer
HARDINESS	Frost tender
FLOWERING	Summer to autumn

'Ellen White'

E

THERE'S SOMETHING CHARMING about creamy white fuchsias, and 'Ellen White' is an exceptional, trailing one. It has large, fully double blooms with a sumptuously pleated and ruffled, creamy white corolla that is balanced by the slender, elongated sepals (initially lime green, they mature to white with a hint of pink). These, incidentally, develop a pink blush on their tips as they mature to match the tube. With early pinching out, the plant will thicken up and develop a nicely rounded shape which is perfect for a hanging basket.

PLANT PROFILE	
HEIGHT 10–12in (25–30cm)	
SPREAD 12in (30cm)	
HABIT Lax, trailing	
HARDINESS Frost hardy	
FLOWERING Summer	

E

'Empress of Prussia'

HARDY RED FUCHSIAS ARE ALWAYS POPULAR and 'Empress of Prussia', which was introduced in the late 19th century, remains one of the best. The plant's vigorous, upright stems are covered with flowers, with six to eight bright red blooms produced at every leaf joint. The Empress can be used as a flowering hedge or to edge a path; it also goes well with ornamental grasses and provides much-needed height in a border. To guard against frost damage in cooler zones, cover the crowns with a thick layer of shredded bark.

PLANT PROFILE

HEIGHT 3ft (1m)

SPREAD 3ft (1m)

HABIT Upright bush

HARDINESS Fully hardy

FLOWERING Summer

'Estelle Marie'

E

SHORT, BUSHY, AND COMPACT, this fuchsia has the ideal
qualities for a successful container plant. However, if you
prefer to use your fuchsias as bedding, 'Estelle Marie' is more
than capable of holding its own in a busy summer border—
plant it at the front, though, because of its short stature. The
exquisite flowers are made up of greenish white sepals and
tube and a violet-blue corolla that darkens slightly as it ages.
Unusually, the flowers are held upright on stiff stems above the
dark green foliage.

PLANT PROFILE

HEIGHT 12–18in (30–45cm)

SPREAD 12–18in (30–45cm)

HABIT Upright, compact bush,
self-branching

HARDINESS Z9–11 H12–9

FLOWERING Summer to first frost

E | 'Eternal Flame'

A SHOWY, PALE PINK AND ORANGE FUCHSIA, 'Eternal Flame'
is a reliable and heavy summer flowerer. It makes an excellent
plant to front a group of fuchsias in a courtyard or cottage
garden, and its colors would be perfect in a Mediterranean-
style garden in which the floor has been paved with terracotta
tiles. To encourage flowering and the production of new
shoots low down on the bush, keep pinching out the growing
tips in spring and the first half of summer. Given a little extra
heat, this cultivar can be encouraged to continue flowering
over the winter.

PLANT PROFILE

HEIGHT 12–15in (30–38cm)

SPREAD 15–18in (38–45cm)

HABIT Upright bush

HARDINESS Half hardy

FLOWERING Summer to first frost

'Eureka Red'

E

IF YOU'VE BEEN LOOKING FOR A STRONG RED fuchsia to fill
a hanging basket, this recent North American introduction
could be what you've been waiting for. Although not yet
widely available, it is easy enough to track down through a
specialist fuchsia nursery. The lax trailing stems are heavily hung
with flowers that have dark pinkish red and white sepals and
tube, with a pinkish red corolla. When the basket is hung
against a white background, the colors are simply stunning.

PLANT PROFILE

HEIGHT	9–12in (23–30cm)
SPREAD	15–18in (38–45cm)
HABIT	Trailing
HARDINESS	Half hardy
FLOWERING	Summer to first frost

E

'Eva Boerg'

A MULTIPURPOSE FUCHSIA that, thanks to a combination of bushy growth and stems that are on the lax side, can be grown in a pot, hanging basket, or even trained as a mini-standard. In mild areas, it can be left growing in the border all year as a low-growing shrub (protect it against severe frost by covering the crown with a thick layer of shredded bark). There is never a shortage of its pinkish white and pinkish purple, single to semidouble flowers. The leaves are soft, light green with serrated edges.

PLANT PROFILE

HEIGHT 18in (45cm)

SPREAD 24–36in (60–90cm)

HABIT Lax, low bush or trailing

HARDINESS Frost hardy

FLOWERING Summer to autumn

'Evensong'

APART FROM A TOUCH OF PINK ON THE TUBE, the bell-shaped flowers of this cultivar are almost entirely white. This makes it a useful addition to a collection of fuchsias, since it will blend in with any other color scheme. For maximum effect, it is best planted in dappled shade where the pale blooms will have greater impact. As they age, the flower shape loosens and the sepals curl upward. 'Evensong' makes a neat, compact bush that is ideal for containers or the front of a summer border.

E

PLANT PROFILE

HEIGHT 18–24in (45–60cm)

SPREAD 12in (30cm)

HABIT Upright, compact bush, self-branching

HARDINESS Half hardy

FLOWERING Summer to first frost

F

'Fascination'

THE FANCIFUL, FRILLY FLOWERS of 'Fascination' are made
up of a red tube and sepals with a pink corolla that carries red
veining. An abundance of flowers on vigorous growth makes it
a very appealing fuchsia that will look good as the centerpiece
in a large pot. Surround it with trailing pelargoniums and
small-leaved ivies that tumble over the sides, or plant it in
the summer border next to the white, daisylike flowers of a
marguerite. Although easy to grow, it will need regular feeding
with a nitrogen-rich fertilizer. In old gardening books it is
sometimes listed as 'Emile de Wildeman'.

PLANT PROFILE

HEIGHT 18–24in (45–60cm)

SPREAD 12–15in (30–38cm)

HABIT Upright bush

HARDINESS Half hardy

FLOWERING Summer to first frost

'Fey'

WITH A LITTLE EFFORT, this fuchsia will make a spectacular
show in a hanging basket. The stiff growth needs regular
pinching out to encourage it to trail, but the rewards speak for
themselves. Good basket companions for the waxy white and
porcelain-blue double flowers would be a scarlet fuchsia and
the yellow, daisylike flowers of *Bidens ferulifolia*, which are
produced on long, wiry stems. Plant 'Fey' in an ornamental
urn and it will tumble prettily over the edges, or train it as
a semiweeping standard. A spot in full sun suits it best.

PLANT PROFILE

HEIGHT 12–15in (30–38cm)

SPREAD 15–18in (38–45cm)

HABIT Stiff trailing

HARDINESS Half hardy

FLOWERING Summer to first frost

F | 'Fiona'

'FIONA' IS A GENTLE MIX OF COLORS and the slender, elegant flowers make a refreshing change from the brash, "in-your-face" cultivars that so often hog the limelight. This fuchsia deserves special treatment—plant it in ornate containers and use it to encircle a statue or fountain. Alternatively, grow it in a basket hung from a sturdy pole above a group of shrub roses and annuals. Its vigorous growth is often described as trailing because the lax, spreading stems grow horizontally. Avoid overwatering 'Fiona', since this will make it more susceptible to botrytis.

PLANT PROFILE

HEIGHT 12–15in (30–38cm)

SPREAD 18–24in (45–60cm)

HABIT Bushy, horizontal, lax stems

HARDINESS Half hardy

FLOWERING Summer to first frost

'Flash'

JEWEL-BRIGHT 'FLASH' makes a big impact as a low-growing edging plant for a border or path. The flashy red flowers may be small, but they are produced in such numbers that they almost obscure the pale green foliage. This vigorous fuchsia is hardy in some areas and can be left outside in the border over winter. If severe frost threatens, keep the worst of the cold out by covering the crown with a thick layer of shredded bark.

F

PLANT PROFILE

HEIGHT 3ft (1m)

SPREAD 3ft (1m)

HABIT Upright bush

HARDINESS Z9–11 H12–9

FLOWERING Summer

F | 'Florabelle'

THE GLORIOUSLY COLORFUL RED TUBE and sepals and dark mauve corolla of 'Florabelle' make such an excellent show that it is well worth growing alone as a feature. A trailing fuchsia, its flexible, lax stems give a relaxed and informal look, and the single blooms are produced in abundance, making it ideal for hanging baskets.

PLANT PROFILE

HEIGHT 18in (45cm)

SPREAD 15–18in (38–45cm)

HABIT Trailing

HARDINESS Half hardy

FLOWERING Summer to first frost

'Foxgrove Wood'

'BUSHY WOOD' WOULD BE A BETTER NAME because the growth
is exceptionally full. A neat, upright shape makes 'Foxgrove
Wood' perfect for a large container, while it is also just tall
enough to be used as a centerpiece in the middle of an early
summer bedding plan. The flower colors—pink tube and
sepals with blue corolla—combine well with reds and white,
and blend into a wide variety of color schemes. An early
flowering cultivar, it will put on a good show while the buds
of other fuchsias are still tightly closed.

PLANT PROFILE

HEIGHT 24–30in (60–75cm)

SPREAD 24–30in (60–75cm)

HABIT Upright bush

HARDINESS Borderline frost hardy

FLOWERING Summer

F | 'Frau Hilde Rademacher'

THIS SLIGHTLY FLOPPY, SPREADING FUCHSIA will complement more upstanding cultivars as part of a large display. Introduced from Germany in the mid-1920s, the petals of the corolla form a tight ball under the winglike sepals. The effect from a distance is of a swarm of exotic insects hovering over the plant. Use this fuchsia in hanging baskets or squeeze it into a large container where the adjacent plants will help keep it upright and stop it from sprawling.

PLANT PROFILE

HEIGHT 18–24in (45–60cm)

SPREAD 18–24in (45–60cm)

HABIT Lax bush

HARDINESS Borderline frost hardy

FLOWERING Summer

'Frosted Flame'

A COLORFUL SUBJECT, 'Frosted Flame' combines a white tube and sepals with a flame-colored corolla—shades rich enough to stand out well against white or pale backgrounds. The large barrel-shaped flowers appear in great profusion and will color up best in light shade. It is a useful early flowerer and, as a natural trailer, will quickly fill a hanging basket.

PLANT PROFILE	
HEIGHT 12–15in (30–38cm)	
SPREAD 18–24in (45–60cm)	
HABIT Trailing	
HARDINESS Half hardy	
FLOWERING Summer to first frost	

F | *fulgens*

THIS GOLDEN OLDIE was first introduced from Mexico in 1888. It makes an impressive display in a large planter, with strong, upright growth and clusters of pale red, slender flowers hanging from the extreme ends of the stems. When the blooms fade—they are very long-lasting—they are followed by deep purple fruits. At 9in (23cm) long, the light green, heart-shaped leaves are the largest of any fuchsia. This is one of the easiest of the species to grow, but it must have winter warmth.

PLANT PROFILE

HEIGHT 5ft (1.5m) or more

SPREAD 32in (80cm)

HABIT Upright shrub

HARDINESS Z13–15 H12–9

FLOWERING Summer to autumn

'Garden News'

G

A POPULAR CHOICE that can be relied upon to produce a long season of large, double flowers. These appear mostly in groups of four at each leaf axil (where the leaf joins the stem) on strong, upright stems. It has a hardy constitution and can stay outside all year in mild areas (covering the crown with a thick layer of shredded bark is a good insurance policy). The combination of soft pink and magenta flowers makes it a good mixer in a pastel border. For the best petal color, give it a spot in full sun. Over the years, 'Garden News' has proved itself to be a very reliable cultivar.

PLANT PROFILE

HEIGHT 18–24in (45–60cm)

SPREAD 18–24in (45–60cm)

HABIT Upright, bushy shrub, self-branching

HARDINESS Z9–11 H12–9

FLOWERING Summer to autumn

G | 'Gartenmeister Bonstedt'

THE BRICK RED, LONG, THIN FLOWERS are typical of a fuchsia in the Triphylla group but have one marked difference—a noticeable bulge on the tube. 'Gartenmeister Bonstedt' has a particularly long flowering season, with clusters of blooms appearing into autumn. A strong, erect bush with rich dark bronze-green leaves, it makes a superb feature plant for an ornamental pot on a warm, sunny patio. It is very tender and needs to overwinter at a minimum temperature of 50°F (10°C). Bring it into a heated conservatory or greenhouse at the end of summer, where it will also flower for longer.

PLANT PROFILE	
HEIGHT 18–24in (45–60cm)	
SPREAD 15–18in (38–45cm)	
HABIT Upright bush	
HARDINESS Z8–10	
FLOWERING Summer to autumn	

'Gay Fandango'

G

DELICATE COLORS make this cultivar a valuable plant for a
container garden—the tube and sepals are carmine pink with
a rosy lilac corolla. If you have never grown fuchsias before,
this one would be a good starter plant, since it is reliably
strong and puts on a rewardingly lavish show of flowers. It is
also extremely versatile, and is happy growing in containers,
hanging baskets, and in the summer border. If you want to try
your hand at training, it can be shaped easily into a standard.

PLANT PROFILE

HEIGHT 15–18in (38–45cm)

SPREAD 15–18in (38–45cm)

HABIT Trailing, spreading

HARDINESS Half hardy

FLOWERING Summer to first frost

G | 'Genii'

ONE OF THE FEW ORNAMENTAL HARDY FUCHSIAS, 'Genii'
deserves a place in the border for its foliage color alone. In full
sun the leaves are a pale lime-yellow and are carried on bright
red stems; however, in shade the vibrant tones are quickly lost
and will revert to dull green. Although small and single, the
blooms are freely produced and show an interesting mix of
colors—the sepals and tube are cerise, while the corolla starts
out violet and ages to purple-red. This cultivar grows best
outdoors; in a conservatory or greenhouse it often drops its
buds and flowers.

PLANT PROFILE

HEIGHT 30–36in (75–90cm)

SPREAD 30–36in (75–90cm)

HABIT Upright bush

HARDINESS Z9–11 H12–9

FLOWERING Summer to autumn

'Ginger'

G

COMPACT, BUSHY 'GINGER' is suitable for a wide range of
containers, including patio pots, window boxes, and hanging
baskets. It is one of the fabulous Shadow Dancer cultivars
introduced by German breeder Wolfram Götz. The dainty
salmon pink and white flowers appear in great profusion over
a very long period—from late spring through to the first
frost—and since they are held well above the small leaves, they
make a huge impact despite their diminutive size.

PLANT PROFILE	
HEIGHT 20in (50cm)	
SPREAD 12in (30cm)	
HABIT Compact bush	
HARDINESS Half hardy	
FLOWERING Late spring to first frost	

G | *glazioviana*

THIS IS NOT A HIGH–OCTANE ORNAMENTAL and its small, thin pink flowers are rather understated, but it has a touch of the wild about it and is a good plant for a cottage garden. Although very vigorous, it has a casual, relaxed feel and is a welcome change from some of the frillier cultivars. In many areas it will survive outdoors over winter, although a severe frost will damage the topgrowth. New stems will shoot from the base of the plant in spring, but you would be well-advised to protect the crown with a thick layer of shredded bark.

PLANT PROFILE	
HEIGHT 20in (50cm)	
SPREAD 6ft (2m)	
HABIT Spreading bush	
HARDINESS Hardy	
FLOWERING Summer	

'Golden Dawn'

G

NIP THIS ONE IN THE BUD if you want a more compact, bushy fuchsia, since its stems naturally tend to shoot straight up. While the plant is still young, start pinching out the growing tips to encourage side branching. With a little time and patience it also makes an excellent standard. The single flowers, which appear in huge numbers, are a pleasing blend of salmon pink and orange with just a touch of vibrant fuchsia pink on the corolla to jazz up the color blend.

PLANT PROFILE	
HEIGHT 12–15in (30–38cm)	
SPREAD 12–15in (30–38cm)	
HABIT Upright bush	
HARDINESS Z9–11 H12–9	
FLOWERING Summer to first frost	

G | 'Golden Margaret Roe'

THE DELICATE CREAM AND GREEN VARIEGATION on the foliage of this charming cultivar would be lost in a busy mixed border or among other more strident fuchsias. Grow it either in a container or in a gravel garden where the neutral tones of the stones won't distract the eye. The single flowers are medium-sized and a subtle combination of rosy red and pale violet. In mild areas you may find it will survive outside over winter—covering the crown with a thick layer of shredded bark will help protect it from the cold.

PLANT PROFILE

HEIGHT 12–15in (30–38cm)

SPREAD 12–15in (30–38cm)

HABIT Upright bush

HARDINESS Half hardy

FLOWERING Summer to first frost

'Golden Marinka'

THE MOST POPULAR VARIEGATED CULTIVAR, almost every leaf of 'Golden Marinka' is different from its neighbor. Some are a random blend of green and yellow, while others are nearly all-green or all-yellow, but all carry strong red veining. As with most variegated plants, it colors best in full sun. Not to be upstaged, the flowers are rich red and, although single, they have the appearance of being semidouble. 'Golden Marinka' is best in a hanging basket due to its trailing growth. Frequent pinching out is recommended. Avoid overwatering, which makes the plant susceptible to botrytis.

PLANT PROFILE	
HEIGHT 16–12in (5–30cm)	
SPREAD 12–18in (30–45cm)	
HABIT Trailing	
HARDINESS Z9–11 H12–9	
FLOWERING Summer to first frost	

G | 'Golden Treasure'

VARIEGATED FOLIAGE IS THIS FUCHSIA'S KEY selling point, since the purple and scarlet flowers are not especially attractive, a trifle sparse, and late to appear. The leaves, which are a colorful blend of pale golden green and yellow with red veining, make a lively backdrop to the flowers and those of adjacent plants. The leaves have a tendency to lose their variegation, so shoots with all-green foliage should be cut out as soon as they appear. 'Golden Treasure' is more a backing plant than a main feature, but it makes a very attractive low-growing edging plant to grace the front of the border.

PLANT PROFILE

HEIGHT 15–18in (38–45cm)

SPREAD 24–30in (60–75cm)

HABIT Low-growing bush

HARDINESS Half hardy

FLOWERING Summer to first frost

'Gordon Thorley'

G

A THOROUGHLY ATTRACTIVE FUCHSIA that is well worth tracking down, although you may have to go to a specialist nursery. The flowers have bright pink, winglike sepals, and a white corolla with intense red veining. The color combination is given a boost by the dark green leaves. 'Gordon Thorley' makes an attractive and shapely container plant and is also an exceptional summer bedder.

PLANT PROFILE

HEIGHT 18in (45cm)

SPREAD 24in (60cm)

HABIT Upright bush, self-branching

HARDINESS Borderline hardy

FLOWERING Summer to first frost

G | 'Graf Witte'

THIS LATE-19TH-CENTURY FRENCH FUCHSIA is perfectly hardy
and can be left in a sunny border all year in milder regions,
where it would look wonderful grown as a low, informal
hedge. The bell-shaped flowers, which are small, single, and
abundant, are a subtle mix of red with bluish red and held on
upright, branching growth. The leaves are unusual, displaying a
touch of yellow with a crimson midrib and veining.

PLANT PROFILE

HEIGHT 24–36in (60–90cm)

SPREAD 24–36in (60–90cm)

HABIT Bush

HARDINESS Fully hardy

FLOWERING Summer

'Grand Prix'

G

A PROLIFIC FLOWERER, 'Grand Prix' has white tubes and sepals with plump, double rosy violet corollas. A superb and plentiful show of blooms coupled with bushy growth makes it a good choice for containers and the front of a border, where it will mix well with annuals and other fuchsias. In larger planting plans, its strong, upright habit makes it an extremely useful filler for any gaps.

PLANT PROFILE

HEIGHT 12–15in (30–38cm)

SPREAD 12–15in (30–38cm)

HABIT Upright bush

HARDINESS Half hardy

FLOWERING Summer to first frost

G | 'Grayrigg'

AN OUTSTANDING HARDY FUCHSIA, 'Grayrigg' falls into the useful pastel color category, which means it can be slotted into most border plans. The blush sepals are tipped in green, while the eggshell-blue corolla is faintly veined with pink. The single flowers will best retain their pale splendor if given a spot in light shade—strong sun intensifies the pigment. This cultivar is reliably hardy in many areas and is suitable for growing as a low, permanent hedge.

PLANT PROFILE

HEIGHT	36in (90cm)
SPREAD	36in (90cm)
HABIT	Upright bush
HARDINESS	Fully hardy
FLOWERING	Summer

'Grumpy'

G

NOT IN THE LEAST BIT GRUMPY, this jolly colored fuchsia is a combination of bright pink and navy blue. The small single flowers appear in large numbers right through summer on outward-pointing stems. It is a good subject for the hardy border where, in mild gardens, it can be left outside in winter. 'Grumpy' is a dwarf cultivar and must be placed toward the front of any planting plan or it will be overshadowed by taller plants. Try growing it in a series of matching pots to line a driveway or to surround a special garden feature, such as a bird bath or statue.

PLANT PROFILE

HEIGHT 9–12in (23–30cm)

SPREAD 9–12in (23–30cm)

HABIT Prostrate bush, self-branching

HARDINESS Borderline hardy

FLOWERING Summer

H | 'Happy Fellow'

A SUITABLY CHEERY COLOR COMBINATION of light orange and
smoky rose makes 'Happy Fellow' a good choice for injecting
zing into the late-summer garden. A prolific flowerer with an
unusual pleated corolla, it provides a steady trickle of color
through until autumn. Use it to complement cannas and
dahlias in a hothouse border to keep things sizzling until the
first frosts. In mild areas you can risk leaving it outside over
winter (cover the crown with a thick layer of shredded bark).
If you prefer to bring it in under cover, wait until midautumn
to eke out the last of the flowers.

PLANT PROFILE

HEIGHT	18in (45cm)
SPREAD	12–15in (30–38cm)
HABIT	Upright bush
HARDINESS	Half hardy
FLOWERING	Summer to first frost

'Happy Wedding Day'

H

BRED IN AUSTRALIA IN 1985, 'Happy Wedding Day' is an obvious choice of name when you see the heavy white blooms edged faintly in pink. The flowers are exceptionally large and, considering their size, produced fairly freely. *En masse* they can sometimes become too heavy for the stems and will need some support. The mid-green leaves have serrated edges. Although described as a bush fuchsia, the stems are rather lax, bordering on trailing, making it ideal for a hanging basket. Early pinching out will help to keep it shapely.

PLANT PROFILE

HEIGHT 18–24in (45–60cm)

SPREAD 15–18in (38–45cm)

HABIT Lax bush or stiff trailing

HARDINESS Half hardy

FLOWERING Summer to first frost

H 'Harry Gray'

PINK AND WHITE POWDER PUFFS is an apt description of the double flowers of this modern cultivar. They appear in such large numbers that they completely obscure the dark green foliage. Short, wiry, red stems and a lax, trailing habit make it an exceptional plant for a hanging basket—some growers regard it as one of the best basket fuchsias of all time. Growth is dense, and a basket is soon filled to the brim. It can also be planted in a large tub, where its stems will happily tumble over the sides.

PLANT PROFILE

HEIGHT 9–12in (23–30cm)

SPREAD 12–18in (30–45cm)

HABIT Trailing, self-branching

HARDINESS Z9–11 H12–9

FLOWERING Summer to first frost

hatschbachii

FOR SOMETHING COMPLETELY DIFFERENT, consider growing
F. hatschbachii. Small, single flowers—red tube and sepals with
violet corolla—are produced on precariously thin, wiry
growth that needs propping up on sticks. Not really suited to
the confines of a container, it is happiest in a cottage garden
border where it is free to sprawl and develop into an anarchic,
tumbling pile of flowers and stems. It isn't a neat plant by any
means, but it is a conversation-starter.

PLANT PROFILE

HEIGHT 30–40in (75–100cm)

SPREAD 40in (100cm)

HABIT Wiry bush

HARDINESS Frost hardy

FLOWERING Summer

H | 'Hawkshead'

'Hawkshead'

A HARDY WHITE FUCHSIA, 'Hawkshead' makes plenty of tough, shrubby, upright growth and is a great improvement on its parent plant, *F. magellanica* var. *molinae*. Plant it in beds and borders to enhance a white plan, or create a lively contrast by placing it next to a scarlet fuchsia, such as 'Riccartonii'. It can be left outside all year in some areas, but provide a covering of shredded bark over the crown to keep out the worst of the cold. If the topgrowth gets cut down by a hard frost, the plant will quickly shoot up in spring, with stems reaching up to 4ft (1.2m) on the current year's growth.

PLANT PROFILE

HEIGHT 4ft (1.2m)

SPREAD 3ft (90cm)

HABIT Upright bush

HARDINESS Fully hardy

FLOWERING Summer

'Heidi Ann'

ALTHOUGH NOT COMPLETELY HARDY, it is safe to leave this fuchsia in the border over winter in mild, sheltered gardens. The brightly colored, double flowers have frilly skirts, with numerous tiny petals (known as petaloids) surrounding the corolla. The blooms are freely produced from quite early in the season and look particularly handsome with the crimson-ribbed, dark green leaves. 'Heidi Ann' has thick, bushy growth and makes a strong feature in a small container. It also works well as an edging plant for the front of a border or along a path. Early pinching out is recommended.

PLANT PROFILE
HEIGHT 15–18in (38–45cm)
SPREAD 18–24in (45–60cm)
HABIT Compact, upright bush, self-branching
HARDINESS Frost hardy
FLOWERING Summer

H | 'Heidi Weiss'

UNASHAMEDLY FRILLY, THE FLOWERS of this cultivar look like fancy meringues. The double corolla, which is white with scarlet veining, flares out under a crown of rose red sepals. The blooms appear on upright, bushy stems among the small, dark green leaves. Pinch out the stems in spring and early summer to promote new growth lower down and create an even more flowery effect. Grow flamboyant 'Heidi Weiss' as a feature plant in a container or an island bed, where it will happily hog the limelight. It is a sport (a mutation occurring in a bud that develops into a new plant) of 'Heidi Ann'.

PLANT PROFILE

HEIGHT 12–24in (30–60cm)

SPREAD 12–24in (30–60cm)

HABIT Upright bush, self-branching

HARDINESS Z9–11 H12–9

FLOWERING Summer to first frost

'Herald'

AN OLD AND FREE–FLOWERING FUCHSIA that remains as popular today as when it was first introduced over 100 years ago. Although the flowers are classic fuchsia colors, they are in soft, subtle tones, with red tube and sepals and a corolla that matures from bluish purple to reddish purple. This cultivar's upright shape makes it an unmissable feature plant in an ornamental pot. Use its rich colors to brighten up a dull courtyard or patio, especially where the walls are white.

H

PLANT PROFILE

HEIGHT 24–36in (60–90cm)

SPREAD 24–36in (60–90cm)

HABIT Upright bush, self-branching

HARDINESS Frost hardy

FLOWERING Summer

H | 'Hermiena'

DUE TO ITS BRANCHING, TRAILING STEMS, this little-known
Dutch cultivar is nearly always grown in a hanging basket or
pot, where it makes an exquisite show. Its highly distinctive,
neatly furled plum corolla peeks out from an overhang of
white sepals flushed pink. Although the single flowers are on
the small size, the fuchsia is very floriferous and highly rated.

PLANT PROFILE

HEIGHT 6–12in (15–30cm)

SPREAD 12–18in (30–45cm)

HABIT Trailing, self-branching

HARDINESS Half hardy

FLOWERING Summer to first frost

'Heron'

H

A VERY IMPRESSIVE FUCHSIA with bright red tube and sepals and a violet-blue corolla streaked with red. If you pinch back new growth in spring and early summer you can turn an abundance of single flowers into a veritable avalanche. Bolt upright and very sturdy, 'Heron' makes a good accent plant for the summer border or the main event in a patio planter. Easy to grow, it's a good choice for someone starting a collection of fuchsias, and its distinctive looks make it a must-have for any fuchsia lover.

PLANT PROFILE

HEIGHT 24–36in (60–90cm)

SPREAD 3–4ft (1–1.2m)

HABIT Upright bush, self-branching

HARDINESS Frost hardy

FLOWERING Summer to first frost

H | 'Hidcote Beauty'

VERY POPULAR BECAUSE OF ITS GENTLE COLORS, 'Hidcote Beauty' has a waxy cream tube and green-tipped sepals with a salmon pink corolla and soft green foliage. The flowers are produced freely and the habit is a winning combination of gracefulness and vigor, making it suitable for most purposes. With careful training it makes a good standard, or plant it in a hanging basket or bedding plan.

PLANT PROFILE

HEIGHT 15–18in (38–45cm)

SPREAD 12–15in (30–38cm)

HABIT Upright bush, self-branching

HARDINESS Half hardy

FLOWERING Summer to first frost

'Hinnerike'

ORANGE IS A USEFUL COLOR IN THE GARDEN, and the flowers of 'Hinnerike' are in a particularly lively shade. Not to be outdone, the glossy green leaves carry red veining and the stems are a cool grayish green. Strongly upright but rather stiff, this fuchsia needs regular pinching out to help it develop a good rounded shape—this will also boost the production of flowers. Plant it in a large pot or tub to make it easier to bring under cover over winter, and in summer place the container in bright light to prevent both the leaves and flowers from losing their strong tones.

PLANT PROFILE

HEIGHT 30–36in (75–90cm)

SPREAD 18–24in (45–60cm)

HABIT Upright bush

HARDINESS Half hardy

FLOWERING Summer to first frost

H | 'Holly's Beauty'

WHITE AND ORANGE SOUNDS ZINGY but the double flowers of 'Holly's Beauty' are in muted rather than citrus tones, and even the white sepals are softened with a flush of pale rose. The leaves too are in soft rather than vibrant green. The colors work well together, however, and it makes a lovely subject for a hanging basket, where its naturally trailing stems are free to tumble at will.

PLANT PROFILE

HEIGHT 9–12in (23–30cm)

SPREAD 15–18in (38–45cm)

HABIT Trailing

HARDINESS Half hardy

FLOWERING Summer to first frost

'Hollywood'

A SUITABLY GLAMOROUS CULTIVAR with over-the-top double blooms in crimson and white. When flowers are this large, they are rarely produced in great numbers, but 'Hollywood' won't disappoint anyone, since it can be relied upon to put on a great performance. It makes a lovely upright bush which, if you allow it, will hog the limelight in any summer border.

H

PLANT PROFILE

HEIGHT 18–24in (45–60cm)

SPREAD 12–15in (30–38cm)

HABIT Upright bush

HARDINESS Half hardy

FLOWERING Summer to first frost

H | 'Howlett's Hardy'

UNUSUALLY FOR A HARDY FUCHSIA, this one has fairly large blooms. A reliable source of strong color in the early summer garden, the freely produced, bell-shaped blooms have a rich violet-purple corolla and, in wonderful clashing contrast, a scarlet tube and sepals. Growth is strong, upright, and bushy and, if given a sunny site, this tough old fuchsia (which is hardy in many areas) can be left in the border all year. Try growing it as a low, informal hedge.

PLANT PROFILE

HEIGHT 24–30in (60–75cm)

SPREAD 24–30in (60–75cm)

HABIT Upright bush

HARDINESS Fully hardy

FLOWERING Early summer

'Huntsman'

SUBTLE, SOFT PASTEL 'HUNTSMAN' is worth its weight in gold when you need to cool down a bed of brash summer colors or perk up a pastel plan that's looking a little washed out. As fuchsias go, this is really the perfect backup plant—you can use it almost anywhere. The plant has a graceful airiness, thanks to the way its flowers hang in open clusters from the slenderest of stems.

PLANT PROFILE	
HEIGHT 15–18in (38–45cm)	
SPREAD 12–15in (30–38cm)	
HABIT Upright bush	
HARDINESS Half hardy	
FLOWERING Summer to first frost	

J

'Jack Acland'

GROW 'JACK ACLAND' IN A HANGING BASKET to fully appreciate its trailing stems, which are strung with fat buds that open to all-pink, bell-shaped flowers (note that the corolla is initially red before changing color). Although the stems are stiff, they are sufficiently lax to make basket training a fairly simple task. By midsummer you will be rewarded with a plant that may measure up to 5ft (1.5m) across. Alternatively, grow it at the front of a border where it will spill onto an adjacent lawn or path, softening any regimental straight lines. "Acland" is often incorrectly spelled "Ackland."

PLANT PROFILE	
HEIGHT 15–18in (38–45cm)	
SPREAD 5ft (1.5m)	
HABIT Stiff trailing	
HARDINESS Half hardy	
FLOWERING Summer to first frost	

'Jack Shahan'

J

IF YOU LOVE LARGE PINK FLOWERS (and this fuchsia produces masses of them over a long summer period), 'Jack Shahan' will soon become a firm favorite. The lax, trailing stems make it suitable for a hanging basket and for training into a weeping standard. You will need to be diligent about pinching out the growing tips in order to train it into shape. In cooler conditions, growth loses its tendency to sprawl and the plant retains a neat, bushy shape. "Shahan" is often incorrectly spelled "Sharon" or "Sharron."

PLANT PROFILE

HEIGHT 12–18in (30–45cm)

SPREAD 18–24in (45–60cm)

HABIT Trailing

HARDINESS Z9–11 H12–9

FLOWERING Summer to first frost

J | 'Jenny Sorensen'

COMPACT AND NOT TOO VIGOROUS, 'Jenny Sorensen' is an elegant fuchsia that's shown off best when grown as a standard. The single flowers have a rich rose pink tube and sepals tipped with green, while the corolla starts off pale lilac but darkens with age. Each of the furled petals carries a hem of dark violet that changes to cerise. Such a beautiful plant could be forgiven for being difficult, but that's not the case—it is surprisingly easy to grow. It also responds well to training. To preserve the flower color, grow in light, dappled shade.

PLANT PROFILE

HEIGHT 18–24in (45–60cm)

SPREAD 15–18in (38–45cm)

HABIT Upright bush, self-branching

HARDINESS Half hardy

FLOWERING Summer to first frost

'Jim Coleman'

J

THERE'S A CERTAIN JAUNTINESS to 'Jim Coleman', due to the upswept sepals and the way the bell-shaped flowers are held semierect above the foliage. Coupled with dense, vigorous growth, this modern cultivar has a very powerful presence. Regularly pinching out the growing tips in spring and summer will encourage more stems to grow from lower down, giving an even more luxuriant display of foliage and flowers. A superb bushy plant for most garden situations (except a hanging basket), it is also a good fuchsia for training.

PLANT PROFILE

HEIGHT 18–24in (45–60cm)

SPREAD 15–18in (38–45cm)

HABIT Upright bush

HARDINESS Half hardy

FLOWERING Summer to first frost

J | 'Jingle Bells'

A VERY STRIKING CULTIVAR, 'Jingle Bells' has smallish flowers with bright red tubes, broad, winglike sepals, and a white corolla with subtle red veining. The abundant blooms are very showy and deserve a place in a hanging basket positioned to catch the eye. For an instant makeover, hang a pair of baskets on either side of a plain front door.

PLANT PROFILE

HEIGHT	15–18in (38–45cm)
SPREAD	15–18in (38–45cm)
HABIT	Lax bush
HARDINESS	Z8–10
FLOWERING	Summer to first frost

'Joe Kusber'

J

HANDSOME 'JOE KUSBER' IS AN EXCELLENT fuchsia with full and frilly double flowers, in pastel shades, that are produced freely throughout the summer. The foliage is correspondingly large and lush. Growth is on the lax side, and it makes a good subject for a hanging basket; if grown as a bush it will need some support. Flowering is long-lasting and continues into autumn, when the display builds up to a crescendo. Although it puts on a good show in its first year, 'Joe Kusber' improves with age and is guaranteed to impress in its second.

PLANT PROFILE

HEIGHT 12–15in (30–38cm)

SPREAD 18–24in (45–60cm)

HABIT Lax bush

HARDINESS Half hardy

FLOWERING Summer to first frost

J

'Joy Patmore'

"LOVELY IN EVERY WAY" is how 'Joy Patmore' is described by many gardeners and professional growers. Few can deny this fuchsia's good looks and even temperament. It is a strong, upright plant that is very easy to grow. The flowers are freely produced and are in an attractive color mix—waxy white sepals carry a slight pink tinge on their undersides and are brightly contrasted with a carmine corolla. The flowers appear in clusters at the end of arching stems. It makes a good standard or bedding plant for a site in full sun.

PLANT PROFILE

HEIGHT 12–18in (30–45cm)

SPREAD 18–24in (45–60cm)

HABIT Upright bush

HARDINESS Z9–11 H12–9

FLOWERING Summer to first frost

'King's Ransom'

INTRODUCED IN NORTH AMERICA IN THE MID-1950s, 'King's Ransom' has big, fat flower buds that open to reveal a white crown of sepals above a double corolla of imperial purple. Both colors stand out well against the mid-green foliage. Free-flowering 'King's Ransom' should be planted in a stylish container, or at the front of a summer border where it can be seen clearly.

PLANT PROFILE

HEIGHT	24in (60cm)
SPREAD	18in (45cm)
HABIT	Upright bush
HARDINESS	Half hardy
FLOWERING	Summer to first frost

K 'Kit Oxtoby'

THIS FAIRLY RECENT INTRODUCTION (from 1990) is invariably used in hanging baskets, where the rosy pink flowers are free to tumble over the sides on long, trailing stems. However, it also makes a very useful container plant. One suggestion would be to set it among a mixed grouping of plants arranged in a pyramid—use bricks to raise the pots into tiers—with 'Kit Oxtoby' as the focal point in the center. The double flowers, which are produced in great numbers, are worthy of the closest scrutiny—a delicate picotee hem around the petals of the corolla makes an especially attractive feature.

PLANT PROFILE

HEIGHT 15–18in (38–45cm)

SPREAD 18–24in (45–60cm)

HABIT Trailing

HARDINESS Half hardy

FLOWERING Summer to first frost

'Kwintet'

A TOTALLY RELIABLE, free-flowering fuchsia, with upright, bushy growth that makes a strong show in a pot or a summer border. The richly colored flowers have rose pink sepals that flex back like wings over the rose red, bell-shaped corolla. These pink tones are carried onto the pistil and stamens. The flowers, which are produced in abundance, start to appear in early summer and continue right through until autumn.

PLANT PROFILE

HEIGHT 18–24in (45–60cm)

SPREAD 15–18in (38–45cm)

HABIT Upright bush self-branching

HARDINESS Half hardy

FLOWERING Summer to first frost

L | 'La Campanella'

A BEAUTIFUL, QUICK-GROWING FUCHSIA with scores of small, semidouble flowers that are white, tinged with pink, and royal purple, aging to lavender. Once the plant is established, the growth rate is phenomenal. A wiry plant with compact, bushy growth, with regular pinching out it will turn into a fabulous specimen for a hanging basket or a tall, spacious container. Don't be alarmed by the flower drop—a large plant may shed a dozen or more blooms in a day—since there are always plenty more buds ready to open and fill the gaps. It copes well with strong sun.

PLANT PROFILE

HEIGHT 6–12in (15–30cm)

SPREAD 12–18in (30–45cm)

HABIT Trailing, self-branching

HARDINESS Z9–11 H12–9

FLOWERING Early summer to first frost

'Lady Boothby'

L

VIGOROUS, UPRIGHT 'LADY BOOTHBY' is a colorful character with crimson and blackish purple flowers. In warmer areas it is hardy enough to be left out over winter (with a thick covering of shredded bark), which means it can be treated as a permanent, informal hedge. If frost does nip the topgrowth, cut back stems to the lowest shoots in spring to encourage fresh new growth. A happy coupling would be to grow 'Lady Boothby' with ornamental grasses, whose long stems share the same airy profile. When raised in a greenhouse this fuchsia will surprise you by its willingness to climb.

PLANT PROFILE

HEIGHT 36–48in (90–120cm)

SPREAD 36–48in (90–120cm)

HABIT Upright bush

HARDINESS Z7–10

FLOWERING Summer

L | 'Lady Isobel Barnett'

THE EXTRAORDINARY ABUNDANCE OF FLOWERS covering this bushy fuchsia makes 'Lady Isobel Barnett' look like a giant bouquet. It is one of the most prolific flowerers available, with eight or more buds in each leaf axil (where the leaf joins the stem), and would be a big hit in any arrangement of pot-grown fuchsias. It could also be used as the centerpiece in a hanging basket or trained as a standard. In its first year it will make a sizable plant, requiring only moderate pinching out but always hungry for a good feed. A bright spot, but not in direct sun, will retain the subtle coloration of its petals.

PLANT PROFILE

HEIGHT 15–18in (38–45cm)

SPREAD 12–15in (30–38cm)

HABIT Upright bush self-branching

HARDINESS Half hardy

FLOWERING Summer to first frost

'Lady Kathleen Spence'

A DELICATE, PASTEL-COLORED FUCHSIA which, because of its lax, spreading habit, can be grown in hanging baskets or in containers. The flowers, which have a pinkish white tube, pale rose sepals, and a delicate lavender corolla, appear freely over summer and always give an excellent show. The petal color is better when it's grown in dappled shade, and if the plant is set against a dark background, the pale blooms will show up well.

PLANT PROFILE	
HEIGHT	18–24in (45–60cm)
SPREAD	15–18in (38–45cm)
HABIT	Lax bush
HARDINESS	Half hardy
FLOWERING	Summer to first frost

L

'Lady Thumb'

A DIMINUTIVE FUCHSIA on a scale as small as its parent plant, 'Tom Thumb'. Its short stems bear dainty leaves and an abundance of tiny, semidouble flowers. Very compact and solid, it makes a pretty low hedge or edging plant. For extra height, plant it in a pot or a rockery. 'Lady Thumb' is also an obvious choice for training as a bonsai. In mild gardens, plants can be left outside all year, but it is best to cover the crown with a precautionary winter mulch of shredded bark. One drawback is a tendency to drop its flowers quite quickly, just like its parent.

PLANT PROFILE

HEIGHT 6–12in (15–30cm)

SPREAD 12–18in (30–45cm)

HABIT Dwarf bush

HARDINESS Z9–11 H12–9

FLOWERING Summer to autumn

'Lambada'

AN EARLY-1990S DUTCH INTRODUCTION with perky purple and pink-white flowers that appear nonstop all summer. The plant plumps up into a lovely bushy shape, making it a great gap-filler for most situations in the summer garden. It responds well to pinching out by putting on even thicker growth and producing ever more flushes of flower buds. Although not widely available, 'Lambada' should be easy enough to track down from a specialist nursery.

L

PLANT PROFILE

HEIGHT 12–15in (30–38cm)

SPREAD 12–15in (30–38cm)

HABIT Upright bush

HARDINESS Half hardy

FLOWERING Summer to first frost

L

'Laura'

ALL-OVER ORANGE FLOWERS (slightly darker on the corolla) together with strong, upright growth make 'Laura' a very desirable fuchsia. It is often sold ready-trained as a standard, with a long bare stem topped by a mass of flowers and leaves. The orange flowers of this fuchsia are a mainstay of "hot and tropical" themes, and look particularly striking when planted among late-flowering red and yellow rudbeckias. Rather confusingly, you may find three other Lauras listed; this one was raised in the Netherlands in 1985.

PLANT PROFILE

HEIGHT 18–24in (45–60cm)

SPREAD 18in (45cm)

HABIT Upright bush

HARDINESS Half hardy

FLOWERING Summer to first frost

'Lechlade Gorgon'

L

"THE MANY-HEADED MONSTER" is an apt description of this fascinating fuchsia which, if it has a free root run, will assume triffid proportions in warm conditions. It can grow up to 10ft (3m) in just three years. Instead of fearsome heads, however, it throws out masses of tiny, mauve flowers in loose clusters, similar to a lilac. These are followed by purple-blue berries. The deep green leaves are huge, up to 5in (13cm) long, and are a feature in themselves. It is very happy growing in a pot—just make it a very large one—and will transform any urban garden into a jungle.

PLANT PROFILE

HEIGHT	24–30in (60–75cm)
SPREAD	24–30in (60–75cm)
HABIT	Vigorous shrub
HARDINESS	Frost tender
FLOWERING	Summer

L | 'Lechlade Magician'

GIVE THIS RAMPANT FUCHSIA PLENTY OF SPACE because in a few years it will make a large, bushy plant. 'Lechlade Magician' has strong-colored flowers, each with a rich purple-red tube and sepals, and a deep purple corolla that fades to brownish red. Hardy enough to be left outside all year in many areas, it will quickly make a magnificent flowering hedge and will also give a colorful boost to a flagging late-summer garden.

PLANT PROFILE

HEIGHT 3ft (1m)

SPREAD 3ft (1m)

HABIT Upright bush

HARDINESS Fully hardy

FLOWERING Summer

'Lena'

SUPREMELY VERSATILE AND VERY FREE-FLOWERING, 'Lena' can be trained into almost any shape, including an attractive standard. It is equally happy growing in the border or in pots and hanging baskets. The dominant color of the semidouble flowers is pink—rose-magenta on the corolla with pale pink sepals. In mild areas it can be left outside all year, although a precautionary winter mulch of shredded bark to cover the crown wouldn't hurt. This beautiful fuchsia has remained highly popular since its introduction in 1862.

PLANT PROFILE

HEIGHT 12–24in (30–60cm)

SPREAD 24–30in (60–75cm)

HABIT Bush or trailing

HARDINESS Z9–11 H12–9

FLOWERING Summer to autumn

L | **'Lena Dalton'**

'LENA DALTON' JUSTIFIES ITS POPULARITY, making an impressive
container plant with plenty of bushy, upright growth. The
flowers are abundant and in a pastel combination of pink tube
and sepals, with a clear blue corolla that fades to mauve. The
flowers are fully double, with four cupped petals in the center
encircled by shorter petals. They stand out well against the
small, dark green, red-veined leaves. This cultivar proves its
worth in the garden, having a gentle, softening effect on strong
colors, while its bushiness makes it the perfect all-purpose
gap-filler for the front of a border.

PLANT PROFILE

HEIGHT 15–18in (38–45cm)

SPREAD 15–18in (38–45cm)

HABIT Upright bush

HARDINESS Z8–10

FLOWERING Summer to first frost

'Leonora'

L

ONE OF THE BEST ALL–PINK FUCHSIAS is how 'Leonora' is often described. Produced in huge numbers, the bell-shaped, single flowers are the gentlest of pastel shades. Easy to grow, its upright, vigorous, bushy habit makes it perfect as a half-hardy bedding plant or a tallish standard. 'Leonora' is also well worth growing as the centerpiece in a pastel border or in a terracotta pot on the patio.

PLANT PROFILE

HEIGHT 24–30in (60–75cm)

SPREAD 12–24in (30–60cm)

HABIT Upright bush

HARDINESS Z9–11 H12–9

FLOWERING Summer to first frost

L

'Leverkusen'

CLASSIFIED AS A TRIPHYLLA FUCHSIA, the bright red flowers are shorter than usual and appear individually in the leaf axils (where the leaf joins the stem) as well as in clusters at the ends of the branches. Very free-flowering over an incredibly long period, it is a welcome change from more frilled and furled fuchsias. Growth is bushy and vigorous, although it reacts badly to being moved or any marked changes in atmosphere by dropping its flowers. Try 'Leverkusen' planted in an ornamental container beside a pool, where its reflection will double its impact.

PLANT PROFILE

HEIGHT 15–18in (38–45cm)

SPREAD 12–15in (30–38cm)

HABIT Upright bush

HARDINESS Frost tender

FLOWERING Summer

'Liebriez'

L

THIS HIGHLY RATED GERMAN FUCHSIA has been around since the late 19th century. It has narrow, leathery foliage and small, pale red and pinkish white semidouble flowers that are freely and continuously produced over a long season. 'Liebriez' is hardy in many areas and can be planted as a permanent, low-growing edging plant or to fill a gap in a shrub border. Tolerant of full sun, it will also grow well in a gravel garden or rockery.

PLANT PROFILE

HEIGHT 12–15in (30–38cm)

SPREAD 18–24in (45–60cm)

HABIT Upright bush

HARDINESS Fully hardy

FLOWERING Summer

L

'Little Jewel'

APTLY NAMED, THIS FIRST-RATE PLANT has strikingly colored flowers that look as if they have been polished. The tube and star-shaped sepals are in strong carmine tones, while the corolla is a light purple with carmine markings at the base of the petals. It is a strong grower, with upright, vigorous stems that will attract attention wherever it is planted, be that in the summer border or in a container. 'Little Jewel' also looks at home among Ali Baba pots and Moroccan-style tiles in a Middle Eastern–style setting.

PLANT PROFILE

HEIGHT 18–24in (45–60cm)

SPREAD 18–24in (45–60cm)

HABIT Upright bush

HARDINESS Half hardy

FLOWERING Summer to first frost

'Love's Reward'

L

A ROMANTIC NAME for a fuchsia with delicate, romantic flowers. Compact and bushy, it makes a nicely shaped plant and can also be easily trained as a neat standard. The small to medium-sized single flowers (white tube and sepals and a violet-blue corolla) appear in great numbers over the season. 'Love's Reward' is regarded by many fuchsia experts as being one of the best for small containers.

PLANT PROFILE
HEIGHT 12–18in (30–45cm)
SPREAD 12–18in (30–45cm)
HABIT Compact bush, self-branching
HARDINESS Z9–11 H12–9
FLOWERING Summer to first frost

M | 'Machu Picchu'

ALTHOUGH LISTED AS A BUSH, 'Machu Picchu' performs best as a trailing plant in a hanging basket. The stems are fairly lax and when grown as a bush will need frequent pinching out to encourage a good shape. A basket affords the best vantage point for enjoying the smallish, single, rose and scarlet flowers which are produced over an incredibly long period of up to nine months. The red-veined, mid-green leaves are carried on red stems. A site in full sun will give the colors a real boost.

PLANT PROFILE

HEIGHT 12–24in (30–60cm)

SPREAD 12–24in (30–60cm)

HABIT Lax bush

HARDINESS Half hardy

FLOWERING Early summer to first frost

'Madame Cornélissen'

RED AND WHITE CULTIVARS were a specialty of the Belgian grower Cornélissen, and in 1860 he introduced 'Madame Cornélissen', which many fuchsia lovers now regard as his best. Against a backdrop of handsome dark green foliage, an abundance of small, semidouble blooms are produced throughout the season. Its strong, vigorous, bushy growth makes a good, permanent low hedge—in mild climates this fuchsia will survive outdoors over winter (cover the crown with a thick layer of shredded bark). It also copes well in containers and can be trained as a standard.

PLANT PROFILE

HEIGHT 24–30in (60–75cm)

SPREAD 24–30in (60–75cm)

HABIT Upright bush, self-branching

HARDINESS Z6–10

FLOWERING Summer to autumn

M | *magellanica*

THE HARDIEST OF ALL FUCHSIAS, *F. magellanica* was found in
the wild growing in the cold climate of the southern regions
of South America, down to Tierra del Fuego. Its genes were
used in many crosses by early growers to toughen up their
new plants. The graceful stems of dark green leaves are hung
with slender crimson and purple flowers, which are followed
by oblong-shaped, reddish purple fruit. Strong-growing and
upright, it makes a substantial hedge.

PLANT PROFILE	
HEIGHT 10ft (3m)	
SPREAD 6–10ft (2–3m)	
HABIT Upright bush	
HARDINESS Z4–9	
FLOWERING Summer to autumn	

magellanica var. *gracilis* 'Aurea'

M

THE KEY SELLING POINT OF 'AUREA' is that it has striking, golden-yellow, spear-shaped leaves with crimson veining. The whole plant comes alive in the autumn sun, when the foliage flickers with fiery orange tones. It is also blessed with vibrant red and purple flowers. Like other magellanicas, its informality suits cottage gardens, especially when allowed to erupt from large gaps in paving. Given a spot in full sun and a thick covering of shredded bark, it can be left outside over winter in many regions.

PLANT PROFILE		
HEIGHT 10ft (3m)		
SPREAD 6–10ft (2–3m)		
HABIT Spreading bush		
HARDINESS Fully hardy		
FLOWERING Summer to autumn		

M | *magellanica* var. *gracilis*

A TYPICAL *MAGELLANICA* FUCHSIA, with slender, dainty
scarlet and purple blooms that appear in large numbers on
graceful, arching stems. These are followed by scarlet berries.
Every bit as vigorous as its relations, it can be left in the
ground all year in warmer areas with a protective winter
mulch of shredded bark covering the crown. It is an ideal
plant for a cottage garden, where its informal outline is
perfectly at home, especially by a pond. It can also be planted
as a flowering hedge, reaching a height of up to 5ft (1.5m).

PLANT PROFILE

HEIGHT 5ft (1.5m)

SPREAD 6ft (1.9m)

HABIT Upright bush

HARDINESS Z7–9

FLOWERING Summer

magellanica var. *gracilis* 'Tricolor'

IF YOU LOVE LEAF VARIEGATION, then 'Tricolor' is a good choice. A kaleidoscope of color, its spear-shaped leaves are liberally splashed with creamy white, pink, and green, and carry pinkish red veining. The flowers are equally bright and are a combination of red sepals and purple corollas. Although small and single, they are produced in great numbers late in the season. Tall, vigorous, bushy, and very hardy, 'Tricolor' makes a flamboyant flowering hedge.

PLANT PROFILE

HEIGHT	36in (90cm)
SPREAD	36in (90cm)
HABIT	Upright bush
HARDINESS	Fully hardy
FLOWERING	Summer

M | *magellanica* var. *pumila*

PUMILA IS LATIN FOR "DWARF," which is an accurate
description of this extremely hardy plant. It must be grown
right at the front of any display or it will be swamped by taller
plants, which would be a shame, because its scarlet and mauve
blooms make a great display all summer long. Perfect for the
rock or gravel garden, it can be left outside all year in warmer
areas if the crown is covered with a layer of shredded bark.

PLANT PROFILE

HEIGHT 12–15in (30–38cm)

SPREAD 12–15in (30–38cm)

HABIT Dwarf, upright bush

HARDINESS Fully hardy

FLOWERING Summer

magellanica 'Thompsonii'

A MUCH MORE FORMAL BUSH than most of the Magellanicas, 'Thompsonii' does not have the long-ranging branches of *F. gracilis* or the massive proportions of *F. magellanica* var. *molinae*. It has gray-green foliage, and the profuse but small, single, delicate red and purple flowers make it an attractive feature plant for the center of an island bed or a group of other fuchsias.

PLANT PROFILE	
HEIGHT 36in (90cm)	
SPREAD 24in (60cm)	
HABIT Upright bush	
HARDINESS Fully hardy	
FLOWERING Summer	

M | *magellanica* var. *variegata*

'VARIEGATA' MAKES A VIGOROUS BUSH, albeit on the small side, rarely reaching beyond knee-high. The leaves are the big attraction: they are light green with white edging and appear on rusty brown stems. The red and purple flowers make a lively contrast. 'Variegata' is a good choice for informal cottage gardens, and it can be left in the ground all year in warmer regions if it is given a protective covering of bark chips over the crown in winter.

PLANT PROFILE

HEIGHT 18–24in (45–60cm)

SPREAD 24in (60cm)

HABIT Upright bush

HARDINESS Fully hardy

FLOWERING Summer to autumn

magellanica var. *molinae*

VERY NEARLY ALL WHITE, apart from a gentle lilac flush on the corolla, this fuchsia flowers as freely as *F. magellanica*, and can be planted beside it to make a red, purple, and white summer-flowering hedge. Upright, vigorous, and extremely robust, in warm areas it will get off to a good start and can be expected to reach 4ft (1.2m) in its first year. Gardeners have given it the descriptive name of "maiden's blush," and it is also rather confusingly referred to as *F. magellanica* 'Alba'.

PLANT PROFILE	
HEIGHT 12ft (4m)	
SPREAD 8ft (2.5m)	
HABIT Upright bush	
HARDINESS Z6–9 H9–6	
FLOWERING Summer to autumn	

M | *magellanica* var. *versicolor*

THERE ARE THREE VERY GOOD REASONS for growing *versicolor*. First, the gray-tinged, green foliage is nicely variegated, with creamy colored patches over the leaves—when young they also carry a hint of pink. Second, the small flowers are a vivid mix of bright red and deep purple. And third, it is hardy enough to be left in the ground all year in some areas, but play it safe and cover over the crown with a thick layer of shredded bark to keep out penetrating frost. Wild, informal, and cottage gardens are all ideal settings for this colorful plant.

PLANT PROFILE

HEIGHT 3ft (1m)

SPREAD 4ft (1.2m)

HABIT Upright bush

HARDINESS Z7–9 H12–1

FLOWERING Summer

'Mancunian'

'MANCUNIAN' IS A MID-1980s BRITISH FUCHSIA that is largely all-white, except for pink veining on the corolla and a rose blush on the top of the tube. The double flowers are "parrot beak" types, which accurately describes their unusual pointed shape. Continuous flowering over a long period and a naturally pendent, vigorous growth habit mark it out as an exceptional performer for a hanging basket. A dark background will highlight the flowers perfectly, while planting it in light shade will help to soften the white.

PLANT PROFILE

HEIGHT	15–18in (38–45cm)
SPREAD	24–30in (60–75cm)
HABIT	Trailing, self-branching
HARDINESS	Half hardy
FLOWERING	Summer to first frost

M | 'Mantilla'

A REAL HOTHOUSE FLOWER, give 'Mantilla' a warm, sunny spot and it will put on a magnificent show. Borne in clusters, the red flowers are up to 3½in (9cm) long, and similar to the slender, dangling blooms of a Triphylla fuchsia. 'Mantilla' has long, willowy trailing stems that make it perfect for a hanging basket, where its bronzy foliage will also be shown off. As soon as the evenings start to cool down in the autumn, plants growing outside should be brought into a warm conservatory or greenhouse to overwinter.

PLANT PROFILE

HEIGHT 6–9in (15–23cm)

SPREAD 24–30in (60–75cm)

HABIT Trailing

HARDINESS Frost tender

FLOWERING Summer

'Marcia'

M

A GOOD PLANT FOR MANY DIFFERENT CONDITIONS, red and magenta 'Marcia' is a fuchsia that commands attention. Listed as a Shadow Dancer cultivar, it is noted for its early and profuse flowering, which continues unabated until the first frost. It is fairly cold tolerant and in milder areas it should survive outside over winter with a covering of shredded bark. A neat, compact bush with a strong, upright habit, use it in patio pots and window boxes or as a centerpiece in a hanging basket.

PLANT PROFILE	
HEIGHT	20in (50cm)
SPREAD	14in (35cm)
HABIT	Upright bush
HARDINESS	Half hardy
FLOWERING	Early summer to first frost

M | 'Margaret'

A VERY HARDY FUCHSIA that will cope with the worst of the weather in most areas. If you are looking for a quick-growing hedge, few plants will shoot up as fast as 'Margaret'—it can reach 4ft (1.2m) in a season. If conditions are favorable, in subsequent years it may reach 8ft (2.5m). The red and violet semidouble flowers are large for a hardy fuchsia, and once the plant is established they appear in such numbers that they completely cover the stems.

PLANT PROFILE

HEIGHT	4ft (1.2m)
SPREAD	3ft (1m)
HABIT	Upright bush
HARDINESS	Fully hardy
FLOWERING	Summer

'Margaret Brown'

A RELIABLE CHOICE FOR THE BORDER, 'Margaret Brown' gives one of the best flower-packed displays of any hardy fuchsia. The small, single blooms are produced over a long period in such numbers that the branches are weighed down with them. They make a wonderful display against the light green foliage. Upright and bushy, it grows well in a pot and also makes a colorful low hedge for milder-climate gardens.

PLANT PROFILE

HEIGHT 24–36in (60–90cm)

SPREAD 24–36in (60–90cm)

HABIT Upright bush

HARDINESS Z9–11 H12–9

FLOWERING Summer to autumn

M 'Margery Blake'

A COMBINATION OF SCARLET AND SOLFERINO–PURPLE is how many catalogs describe this cultivar's pretty single flowers (solferino being a purplish red dye that was first produced in the 1850s in the Italian town of the same name). This fuchsia is an early, profuse, and continuous flowerer that forms a lovely, domed, circular bush. In cold areas, cover the crown with a thick layer of shredded bark to keep out the frost.

PLANT PROFILE

HEIGHT 15in (40cm)

SPREAD 18in (45cm)

HABIT Upright bush

HARDINESS Borderline frost hardy

FLOWERING Early summer to first frost

'Marin Glow'

M

ATTRACTIVELY COLORED, 'Marin Glow' has a white tube and sepals with a rich purple corolla that matures to pink-violet. Not only do you get quality—the flowers are beautifully shaped—but you get them in quantity too. 'Marin Glow' is often sold as a ready-trained standard with a huge mop of flowers and leaves on a bare stem. For perfect symmetry, buy two plants to stand sentinel by the front door or to flank a pathway. If you prefer to use this fuchsia as bedding, note that strong sunlight will bleach the purple corolla, so choose a spot for it in light shade.

PLANT PROFILE		
HEIGHT 12–15in (30–38cm)		
SPREAD 9–12in (23–30cm)		
HABIT Upright bush, self-branching		
HARDINESS Half hardy		
FLOWERING Summer to first frost		

M | 'Marinka'

INTRODUCTION IN 1902, 'Marinka' is still one of the best fuchsias for a hanging basket. The beautifully shaped, medium-sized, single flowers in a lush blend of rich reds are often mistaken for semidoubles. The plant is very vigorous, sturdy, and bushy, although if exposed to drafts when the foliage is young, it is easily scorched. The stems have a cascading habit, making them perfect for baskets or for training as a weeping standard.

PLANT PROFILE

HEIGHT 9–12in (23–30cm)

SPREAD 18–24in (45–60cm)

HABIT Trailing

HARDINESS Z9–11 H12–9

FLOWERING Summer to first frost

'Mary'

M

THIS IMPRESSIVE TRIPHYLLA-TYPE FUCHSIA (denoted by its long, thin tube) needs careful handling to give its best. It abhors the cold, requiring warmth at all times, especially over winter. In warm regions, a sunny spot on the patio is fine, but if bad weather rolls in, bring 'Mary' under cover. Overwatering and overpotting must be avoided too. Pander to its whims and it will produce a profusion of scarlet flowers amid handsome sage green leaves with purple veining.

PLANT PROFILE
HEIGHT 12–24in (30–60cm)
SPREAD 12–24in (30–60cm)
HABIT Upright bush
HARDINESS Z9–11 H12–9
FLOWERING Summer to autumn

M | 'Mary Poppins'

A BEAUTIFUL FUCHSIA, 'MARY POPPINS' combines subtle mid-green foliage with pale apricot and orange-vermilion flowers. Such understated tones make it an extremely good mixer—use it in containers or a summer border to pull together an assorted planting of fuchsias, especially strong reds, into a balanced display. When grown against a blue backdrop, such as a painted wall, this cultivar's muted colors stand out well, gaining extra strength and a warm richness.

PLANT PROFILE

HEIGHT 15–18in (38–45cm)

SPREAD 15–18in (38–45cm)

HABIT Upright bush

HARDINESS Half hardy

FLOWERING Summer to first frost

'Maytime'

M

THE LAX, TRAILING STEMS OF 'MAYTIME' bulk up quickly to make a nicely shaped hanging basket plant, even in its first year. In summer, the double blooms, in delicate shades of pink and violet, appear in great numbers, putting on a lavish show. Hang a basket filled with 'Maytime' from a sturdy pole at the back of a border, ideally against a dark green, leafy background or the dark red tints of a copper beech hedge.

PLANT PROFILE		
HEIGHT 12–15in (30–38cm)		
SPREAD 18–24in (45–60cm)		
HABIT Trailing		
HARDINESS Half hardy		
FLOWERING Summer to first frost		

M | 'Memphis Bell'

'MEMPHIS BELL' IS A SHOWY FUCHSIA that will grab your attention in even the busiest of summer borders. Each flower is a distinctive combination of a red tube and sepals and a lavender-blue, single corolla that flares out into an attractive cup shape. The blooms stand out particularly well against the dark green, waxy leaves. With early training, the naturally strong stems will lend themselves to being shaped into a standard or pillar.

PLANT PROFILE

HEIGHT	20–24in (50–60cm)
SPREAD	8–10in (20–25cm)
HABIT	Upright bush
HARDINESS	Half hardy
FLOWERING	Summer to first frost

'Micky Goult'

BEAUTIFUL AND ELEGANT are words that aptly describe this pretty cultivar. The marshmallow pink and white flowers may be small, but they are freely produced in perky, upright clusters held well above the soft green leaves. In fact, before they open, the buds stand almost vertical. This bushy fuchsia has a neat habit that, with regular pinching, will stay very compact, making it an excellent bedding and container plant.

M

PLANT PROFILE

HEIGHT 12–18in (30–45cm)

SPREAD 18–24in (45–60cm)

HABIT Upright bush self-branching

HARDINESS Z9–11 H12–9

FLOWERING Summer to first frost

M | 'Mieke Meursing'

A TOP-QUALITY CULTIVAR that is described by enthusiasts as "the dream fuchsia." Growth is very vigorous, neat, and bushy, with short-jointed stems that don't require staking, since they never sprawl. The plant has a wonderful symmetrical shape due to the large numbers of stems that fire up from the base. It requires little pampering and responds well to pinching; within six months you can expect it to make a good-sized fuchsia. An exceptional bedding plant, it performs best if its roots are in moist shade. It also makes a wonderful container plant or standard.

PLANT PROFILE

HEIGHT 12–24in (30–60cm)

SPREAD 12–24in (30–60cm)

HABIT Upright bush self-branching

HARDINESS Z9–11 H12–9

FLOWERING Summer to first frost

'Minirose'

M

THE EXQUISITE, DAINTY FLOWERS have an immediate appeal, with their purple corollas and beige tubes and sepals. Much too beautiful to tuck away in the border, 'Minirose' should always be positioned right at the front of any display. Its freely produced flowers are perhaps best appreciated when it is grown as a miniature standard. However, since training requires painstaking pinching out, you could save yourself a lot of time and buy one ready-prepared. 'Minirose' is also a good choice for anyone packing a large number of plants into a small space, such as in containers on a balcony or windowsill.

PLANT PROFILE

HEIGHT 18–24in (45–60cm)

SPREAD 15–18in (38–45cm)

HABIT Compact, upright bush

HARDINESS Half hardy

FLOWERING Summer to first frost

M | 'Mission Bells'

A WONDERFUL NORTH AMERICAN INTRODUCTION, its strong, stiffly upright, vigorous stems, with bell–shaped scarlet and rich purple flowers, make it a really punchy fuchsia for the summer border. Ignore suggestions that it can be late to flower because that is only a minor hiccup. Keep pinching out new growth in spring and early summer to guarantee extra leafy, flowery growth, or train it to make a superb standard. If you feed it regularly, the single flowers may thicken up to semidoubles.

PLANT PROFILE

HEIGHT 18–24in (45–60cm)

SPREAD 18–24in (45–60cm)

HABIT Upright bush, self-branching

HARDINESS Half hardy

FLOWERING Summer to first frost

'Molesworth'

M

BRIGHT AND BREEZY, the cherry and white flowers of this cultivar are shown off to perfection in a hanging basket. The blooms are very early and freely produced, while the corolla is exceptionally full, making it almost a "double double." The perfect setting for such a gorgeous basket would be hanging from an arch over a rustic garden gate, or from the end beam of a pergola. A premier basket fuchsia, with sufficient staking 'Molesworth' also performs well as a summer bedding plant and is suitable for training as a standard.

PLANT PROFILE

HEIGHT 6–9in (15–23cm)

SPREAD 12–15in (30–38cm)

HABIT Trailing, lax bush, self-branching

HARDINESS Half hardy

FLOWERING Summer to first frost

M | 'Moonbeam'

SUGARY PINK AND VERY FRILLY it may be, but 'Moonbeam' still packs a punch. It is a strong-growing plant with large, handsome leaves and makes a robust bush or standard. Despite the plant's vigor, you may find you have to support the stems as they become weighed down with flowers, which can measure up to 3in (8cm) across. The coloration of 'Moonbeam' would best suit a cottage garden or a planting of pastel annuals, where it will help to beef up the display.

PLANT PROFILE	
HEIGHT 15–18in (38–45cm)	
SPREAD 18–24in (45–60cm)	
HABIT Upright bush self-branching	
HARDINESS Half hardy	
FLOWERING Summer to first frost	

'Moth Blue'

M

RELAXED, FLEXIBLE STEMS allow 'Moth Blue' to be grown
successfully in a hanging basket, despite the fact that it isn't
the most natural of trailers. It also makes a useful, if informal,
bushy plant that is not overly upright or too floppy. The large,
double flowers, which are freely produced, have a red tube and
narrow sepals teamed with a deep lilac-blue corolla. They look
very handsome growing through the dark green leaves with
their coppery sheen.

PLANT PROFILE

HEIGHT 15–18in (38–45cm)

SPREAD 12–15in (30–38cm)

HABIT Lax bush or trailing

HARDINESS Half hardy

FLOWERING Summer to first frost

M | 'Mr. A. Huggett'

EARLY TO FLOWER and one of the last to finish in autumn, 'Mr. A. Huggett' puts on an outstanding show of scarlet and mauve single blooms. The whole bush, from top to bottom, is usually covered with buds. It is a fairly hardy specimen and in mild areas can be left growing in the border over winter—if a severe frost is forecast, however, a covering of shredded bark would be a wise precaution. Naturally upright and bushy, it requires little pinching to keep it shapely. Although it is happy in light shade, full sun will improve the petal color.

PLANT PROFILE

HEIGHT 24–30in (60–75cm)

SPREAD 24–30in (60–75cm)

HABIT Upright bush, self-branching

HARDINESS Fully hardy

FLOWERING Summer to autumn

'Mrs. Lovell Swisher'

M

THIS EASILY GROWN CULTIVAR makes a good first fuchsia for beginners. A popular combination of pastel pinks, it was raised in the middle of the last century in North America. Almost to compensate for their smallness, the dainty, single blooms appear in huge numbers along the upright stems. Careful pinching will curb any tendency to spindliness and help to develop a nicely shaped bush with a head densely covered with leaves. Its tall, upright habit also lends itself to training as a standard or pillar.

PLANT PROFILE

HEIGHT 18–24in (45–60cm)

SPREAD 12–24in (30–60cm)

HABIT Upright bush

HARDINESS Z9–11 H12–9

FLOWERING Summer to first frost

M | 'Mrs. Popple'

IN THE PREMIER LEAGUE OF HARDY FUCHSIAS, 'Mrs. Popple' is a very vigorous, free-flowering, upright bush. Suitable as a specimen plant for the hardy border, it is, perhaps, best used as a flowering hedge—its rather spreading habit can take up quite a lot of space. The medium-sized flowers—with rich scarlet tubes and sepals, and clashing violet-purple corollas—appear early and in abundance. Even if top growth is cut back by severe frost over winter, it should quickly reshoot from the base in spring. Neaten up the plant by cutting out dead stems.

PLANT PROFILE

HEIGHT	3–3½ft (1–1.1m)
SPREAD	3–3½ft (1–1.1m)
HABIT	Upright bush
HARDINESS	Z7–9 H12–1
FLOWERING	Summer to autumn

'Mrs. W. P. Wood'

M

SUFFICIENTLY HARDY TO BE LEFT OUTSIDE all year in many regions, this fuchsia makes a wonderful shrubby plant that demands a central position in the border—it is far too vigorous for most containers. The small but abundant pale pink and white flowers, in combination with mid-green leaves, would be a calming influence on any busy and boisterous color scheme. Or use its subtle colors to create a quiet oasis in a corner of the garden where there is some dappled shade.

PLANT PROFILE	
HEIGHT 3ft (1m)	
SPREAD 3ft (1m)	
HABIT Upright bush	
HARDINESS Fully hardy	
FLOWERING Summer	

N | 'Nancy Lou'

CLASSICALLY BEAUTIFUL, the soft, gentle colors of 'Nancy Lou' are predominantly pink and white. The exquisite flowers carry green-tipped, upswept sepals that sit like a crown above the frilly, fully double corolla. These large pompon blooms liberally cover the vigorous, upright growth. You may be lucky enough to find a nursery that sells 'Nancy Lou' as a ready-trained standard, or you can grow it as a bushy plant in an ornamental container.

PLANT PROFILE

HEIGHT 15–18in (38–45cm)

SPREAD 15–18in (38–45cm)

HABIT Upright bush

HARDINESS Z9–11 H12–9

FLOWERING Summer to first frost

'Natasha Sinton'

N

ORCHID PINK FLOWERS give this charming cultivar an air of gentleness and calm. It is invaluable in any pastel color scheme and, with stems that spread and trail, 'Natasha Sinton' is also perfect for growing in a hanging basket. Although the mid-green foliage provides a good foil for the blooms, you could, if you wish, boost the contrast by adding rich green ivy-leaved pelargoniums and trailing ivy. Alternatively, to enhance the pink tones of the petals, plant it beside a trailing red fuchsia, such as 'Marinka'.

PLANT PROFILE

HEIGHT 18–24in (45–60cm)

SPREAD 15–18in (38–45cm)

HABIT Trailing

HARDINESS Half hardy

FLOWERING Summer to first frost

N | 'Nellie Nuttall'

FLAMBOYANT 'NELLIE NUTTALL' has starkly contrasting crimson red and crisp white flowers which, although on the small side, make a great impact, since they are produced in vast numbers over a long period. They also have a tendency to point upward, giving the bush a pert, jaunty appearance. With regular pinching, you can create an extremely bushy, free-flowering plant that is very compact. Use it in containers or as an edging plant for the front of a summer border.

PLANT PROFILE

HEIGHT	12–18in (30–45cm)
SPREAD	12–18in (30–45cm)
HABIT	Upright bush
HARDINESS	Z9–11 H12–9
FLOWERING	Summer to first frost

'Neue Welt'

BUSHY AND HARDY, 'Neue Welt' carries an abundance of flowers in an attractive mix of flashy red and dark violet. There are often more than two buds to each leaf axil (where the leaf joins the stem). If grown among vibrantly colored plants, the violet will add a delicate touch, while the red lends punch to predominantly pastel-colored plans. Use 'Neue Welt' to fill gaps in cottage gardens between shrubs that have yet to reach their final spread, but keep it toward the front of the border because it will only grow thigh-high.

N

PLANT PROFILE

HEIGHT 24–30in (60–75cm)

SPREAD 24–30in (60–75cm)

HABIT Upright bush

HARDINESS Fully hardy

FLOWERING Summer

N | 'Nicki's Findling'

A DUTCH INTRODUCTION from the 1990s, 'Nicki's Findling' is a very attractive, bushy cultivar with upward-facing flowers. The small, almost dumpy blooms have rose-colored sepals and tubes with orange-red corollas—an unlikely combination that actually works very well. It is a good choice for a summer border or for patio containers. You may also find this fuchsia listed as 'Nicis' or 'Nikki's Findling'.

PLANT PROFILE

HEIGHT 18–24in (45–60cm)

SPREAD 18–24in (45–60cm)

HABIT Upright bush

HARDINESS Half hardy

FLOWERING Summer to first frost

'Nice 'n' Easy'

A PERFECTLY NAMED FUCHSIA that fulfills its promise of being nice and easy to grow. A deservedly successful British introduction from 1988, it has tricolored, double flowers—a red tube, dark rose sepals tipped with green, and a clear white corolla. Such interesting markings demand close scrutiny, and 'Nice 'n' Easy' is best planted at the front of the border or used to edge a gravel path in a cottage garden. Its neat, erect bushy shape also makes it perfect for containers.

PLANT PROFILE	
HEIGHT	12–15in (30–38cm)
SPREAD	15in (38cm)
HABIT	Upright bush
HARDINESS	Half hardy
FLOWERING	Summer to first frost

N | 'Nicola Jane'

PERFECTLY RELIABLE, 'NICOLA JANE' IS NOTED for its free-flowering habit. Medium-sized blooms combine rosy pink tubes and sepals with bluish pink corollas. A low-growing plant, it is perfect for creating colorful foreground interest and can be used to hide the bare lower stems of shrub roses. The natural growth habit is upright and bushy, but pinching out will vastly improve the shape.

PLANT PROFILE

HEIGHT 12–18in (30–45cm)

SPREAD 12–18in (30–45cm)

HABIT Upright bust

HARDINESS Borderline hardy

FLOWERING Summer

'Olive Smith'

O

THIS INTERESTING, BUSHY FUCHSIA with a neat shape makes a very attractive pot plant. While the clusters of small carmine and crimson flowers aren't as exaggerated as those of many cultivars, what they lack in size they more than make up for in numbers. The upswept sepals also give the blooms a certain perkiness. 'Olive Smith' is a cultivar to consider growing if you are looking for something a little different.

PLANT PROFILE	
HEIGHT	18–24in (45–60cm)
SPREAD	15–18in (38–45cm)
HABIT	Upright bush
HARDINESS	Half hardy
FLOWERING	Summer to first frost

O   'Orange Crush'

BRIGHT, BRASH AND FULL OF ZEST, this fuchsia produces four
flowers at each pair of leaf axils (where the leaf joins the
stem), giving a plentiful supply of color. Blue-glazed pots
make a good setting, as do front-of-the-border locations with
red and yellow flowers. 'Orange Crush' can also be used to
enhance an orange arrangement of cannas, roses such as
'Remember Me', and poppies. A colorful backdrop of
Cotinus coggygria (smoke bush) will ensure that the citrus
tones really stand out.

PLANT PROFILE	
HEIGHT 15–18in (38–45cm)	
SPREAD 15–18in (38–45cm)	
HABIT Upright bush	
HARDINESS Half hardy	
FLOWERING Summer to first frost	

'Orange Crystal'

THE TWO-TONE ORANGE FLOWERS, with just a dash of green on the tips of the sepals, look exceptionally clear and bright. They hang down in profusion among large, mid-green leaves on short-jointed stems. Growth is reliably bushy, but extra leafy, flowering stems can be forced by nipping out the growing tips in spring and early summer. 'Orange Crystal' is a useful pot plant and summer bedder that can be grown in full sun without any risk of its petals fading.

PLANT PROFILE
HEIGHT 18–24in (45–60cm)
SPREAD 15–18in (38–45cm)
HABIT Compact, upright bush, self-branching
HARDINESS Half hardy
FLOWERING Summer to first frost

O 'Orange Mirage'

THE NAME MAY SUGGEST ALL-ORANGE but the tube and sepals are actually salmon pink, while the corolla has a faint rosy blush. The plant's naturally trailing stems make it a lively choice for a hanging basket, although it can also be used in a window box, provided the background color sets off the flowers. With early training, 'Orange Mirage' makes a perfect weeping standard—rather than limply trailing, however, the stems will be held more horizontally.

PLANT PROFILE

HEIGHT 12–15in (30–38cm)

SPREAD 18–24in (45–60cm)

HABIT Trailing

HARDINESS Half hardy

FLOWERING Summer to first frost

'Orient Express'

OF ALL THE FUCHSIAS WITH LONG, thin flowers (known as Triphyllas), this is possibly one of the loveliest. The slender, fluted blooms, which appear in clusters on the end of stiffly upright stems, are an unusual bicolored rose pink and white. The leaves are mid-green with purple undersides. A reluctance to produce stems can be countered with early and frequent pinching out. 'Orient Express' demands attention and should be given a prime location in a pot on the garden table, or by a sunny focal point close to the house.

PLANT PROFILE	
HEIGHT	18–24in (45–60cm)
SPREAD	9in (23cm)
HABIT	Upright bush
HARDINESS	Frost tender
FLOWERING	Summer

O   'Other Fellow'

A DAINTY CULTIVAR with small pastel-colored flowers that
are freely produced among upright, bushy stems. The corolla
is coral pink and the tube and sepals are waxy white. The mid-
green leaves are on a fittingly small scale too, and carry fine
serrations around their edges. 'Other Fellow' makes a beautiful
container plant, a polished standard, or neat summer bedding.
Note that this fuchsia hates being overwatered.

PLANT PROFILE

HEIGHT 12–18in (30–45cm)

SPREAD 12–18in (30–45cm)

HABIT Upright bush
self-branching

HARDINESS Z9–11 H12–9

FLOWERING Summer to first frost

'Palm Springs'

P

EVEN IN ITS FIRST YEAR, 'Palm Springs' will prove a good investment in terms of basket size and flowers produced. One of the California Dreamer group of fuchsias, this cultivar has a trailing habit and dramatic, fully double, large blooms. These appear over a long period from May until the first frosts, guaranteeing a summer-long infusion of color for containers and mixed borders.

PLANT PROFILE	
HEIGHT 6–8in (15–20cm)	
SPREAD 14in (35cm)	
HABIT Prostrate, trailing	
HARDINESS Half hardy	
FLOWERING Early summer to first frost	

P

'Pam Plack'

IF DELICATE PASTELS are your penchant, then this recent introduction will strike the right note with its white and lilac pink flowers that show up exceptionally well against the light green leaves. It is a strong upright sport (a natural mutation) of 'Margaret Brown', which has long proved to be a vigorous, reliable variety. Both plants make plenty of healthy, dense growth and are ideal as a low-growing hedge.

PLANT PROFILE

HEIGHT 2–3ft (60–90cm)

SPREAD 2–3ft (60–90cm)

HABIT Upright bush

HARDINESS Fully hardy

FLOWERING Early summer to first frost

'Papoose'

A LOW–GROWING, FLOPPY BUSH, 'Papoose' is so prolific that it often produces more flowers than foliage. Brightly colored scarlet and dark purple blooms are produced over a long period. It is a good subject for training, and its rather lax stems can be encouraged to trail from a basket or, with careful pinching out and staking, thicken up into a bush. It would also make a handsome half-standard. 'Papoose' is hardy enough to survive outdoors over winter in mild areas if given a thick insulating cover of shredded bark.

P

PLANT PROFILE	
HEIGHT 15–18in (38–45cm)	
SPREAD 3ft (1m)	
HABIT Lax bush, self-branching	
HARDINESS Frost hardy	
FLOWERING Summer to autumn	

P

'Patio Princess'

DEVELOPED ESPECIALLY FOR CONTAINERS, the double white and rose flowers of 'Patio Princess' appear early and, if you look closely, you will see rose veining on the corolla and leaves. Combine 'Patio Princess' with other pastels or richer, contrasting colors for a wonderful display. Its strong, upright, slender stems make it ideal for training as a standard.

PLANT PROFILE

HEIGHT 15–18in (38–45cm)

SPREAD 15–18in (38–45cm)

HABIT Upright bush, self-branching

HARDINESS Half hardy

FLOWERING Summer to first frost

'Peachy'

SINCE BEING INTRODUCED in North America in 1992, 'Peachy' has become a popular ingredient in hanging baskets. The flowers are an attractive blend of peach shades—the tube and upward-curving sepals have pale salmon tints, while the corolla opens to a lavender pink but ages to light peach. An extra row of small petals, called petaloids, plumps up the skirts of the double corolla.

P

PLANT PROFILE

HEIGHT 15–18in (38–45cm)

SPREAD 18–24in (45–60cm)

HABIT Trailing

HARDINESS Half hardy

FLOWERING Summer to first frost

P

'Peggy King'

As a low-growing, flowering hedge, 'Peggy King' is hard to beat. Upright, bushy growth is soon covered with small rose red and purple flowers that stand out well against the mid-green foliage. For such a strong-growing plant it is surprisingly happy when kept in a container—just make sure it's a large one. 'Peggy King' is considered hardy in many regions and can be left in the ground over winter. Keep out the frost by spreading a thick layer of shredded bark over the crown.

PLANT PROFILE

HEIGHT 30in (75cm)

SPREAD 3ft (1m)

HABIT Upright bush

HARDINESS Frost hardy

FLOWERING Summer

'Peppermint Stick'

P

GOOD-NATURED AND EASY TO GROW, this free-flowering
fuchsia is high up on the list of most experts' top cultivars. You
can use it almost any way you choose (although you will have
a struggle coercing its strong, upright stems to trail) and it will
always give an excellent display. The mid-green leaves are
particularly long and slender. Aptly named 'Peppermint Stick',
the flowers are a strong blend of pinks with some interesting
markings: the corolla is dipped in the deepest purple and, just
like a stick of candy, the sepals have white stripes.

PLANT PROFILE

HEIGHT 18–30in (45–75cm)

SPREAD 18–30in (45–75cm)

HABIT Upright bush,
self-branching

HARDINESS Z9–11 H12–9

FLOWERING Summer to first frost

P | 'Phénoménal'

POPULAR IN VICTORIAN TIMES, this large-flowered, vigorous fuchsia is still a big seller today. Scarlet tube and sepals and rich indigo-blue corolla are an attractive mix that is nicely highlighted by fresh green leaves. The plant puts on such a lavish show that its strong, upright stems bend under the weight and staking may be required. If planted out in a border over summer, sandwich it between a couple of sturdy plants to help support the stems. Although the blooms have a tendency to drop, it is often used in flower arrangements. This fuchsia certainly lives up to its name.

PLANT PROFILE

HEIGHT 18in (45cm)

SPREAD 24in (60cm)

HABIT Upright bush

HARDINESS Half hardy

FLOWERING Summer to first frost

'Phyllis'

AN IDEAL BEGINNER'S STANDARD, 'Phyllis' is easy to grow and can be trained in just one season. The stiff, upright growth is vigorous and, in mild areas, will also make a quick-growing, free-flowering hedge. If you like your fuchsias to have a thick, bushy shape, however, this one will never fit the bill, no matter how much effort you put into pinch-training. Unusually, the sepals of the small rose and cerise flowers occasionally have six or seven points instead of the usual four.

P

PLANT PROFILE	
HEIGHT	3–5ft (1–1.5m)
SPREAD	30–36in (75–90cm)
HABIT	Upright bush
HARDINESS	Z9–11 H12–9
FLOWERING	Summer to autumn

P | 'Pinch Me'

DO JUST AS ITS NAME PROMPTS and this first-rate cultivar will
thicken up beautifully. Grown in a hanging basket, its
abundant trailing stems drip with pairs of very full, double,
white and rich blue-purple flowers. 'Pinch Me' also makes a
wonderful summer bedding plant, but make sure it has ample
space to spread its stems. This fuchsia is noted for staying in
flower for a long period.

PLANT PROFILE

HEIGHT 18–24in (45–60cm)

SPREAD 18–24in (45–60cm)

HABIT Trailing, bushy

HARDINESS Half hardy

FLOWERING Summer to first frost

'Pink Fantasia'

A TOP-QUALITY FUCHSIA that is vigorous, upright, and bushy.
The flowers, which appear in great numbers over the season,
have a pink tube and sepals and a vibrant mauve corolla. Look
closely and you will see that the petals of the corolla have a
dainty picotee edging. The blooms are carried mainly at the
tips of the stems and are held erect above the dark green
leaves, giving the plant a lively appearance.

P

PLANT PROFILE	
HEIGHT 15–18in (38–45cm)	
SPREAD 15–18in (38–45cm)	
HABIT Upright bush	
HARDINESS Z9–11 H12–9	
FLOWERING Summer to first frost	

P | 'Pink Fascination'

THE TWO-TONE FLOWERS have a red tube and sepals teamed with a purple, cup-shaped corolla. They appear on bushy, upright growth with highly distinctive, lemon-edged leaves. This cultivar is good for growing in containers and makes a movable feast for the patio or gravel garden. Pinch out the growing tips in spring and early summer to encourage the plant to throw out even more flowering stems. In some catalogs it is listed under the name of 'Colne Fantasy'.

PLANT PROFILE

HEIGHT 18–24in (45–60cm)

SPREAD 15–18in (38–45cm)

HABIT Upright bush

HARDINESS Half hardy

FLOWERING Summer to first frost

'Pink Galore'

P

A BEAUTIFUL CANDY PINK CULTIVAR with a full, double corolla and long, upswept sepals lightly tipped with green. Its long trailing stems are ideal for a hanging basket, although it doesn't make a large plant and you will need two or three in a basket to give a full, rounded shape. The foliage is particularly attractive; when young, the glossy, dark green leaves have red stems. 'Pink Galore' can also be trained as a weeping standard or used as a summer bedder, but plant it out of direct sunlight to preserve the petal color. As with many trailers, the flowers appear at the end of the stems.

PLANT PROFILE

HEIGHT 9–12in (23–30cm)

SPREAD 18–24in (45–60cm)

HABIT Trailing

HARDINESS Z9–11 H12–9

FLOWERING Summer to first frost

P 'Pink Goon'

A REAL EXTROVERT, 'Pink Goon' is a must-have for those who like their fuchsias upright, bushy, vigorous, and with huge, plump flowers. Each bloom has a red tube and sepals teamed with an apple blossom pink, fully double corolla. However you use it in the garden, it naturally asserts itself as the focal point of any display; it is particularly suitable for a large ornamental pot. It is surprisingly tough and, if given a protective mulch of shredded bark, is able to withstand a winter outdoors in many areas.

PLANT PROFILE

HEIGHT 18–24in (45–60cm)

SPREAD 3ft (1m)

HABIT Upright, bushy

HARDINESS Frost hardy

FLOWERING Summer

'Pink Pearl'

P

A BEAUTIFUL ALL-PINK FUCHSIA, 'Pink Pearl' is very easy to grow and well worth including in any pastel plan. It also makes a perfect pillar or standard and is a good fuchsia for beginners. If you can't find it in the catalogues, try looking under 'Mrs Friedlander'. A former employee of the grower George Bright, she so admired this particular cultivar that he renamed it after her. Incidentally, Bright was the son-in-law of the famous Victorian fuchsia grower James Lye.

PLANT PROFILE

HEIGHT	12–15in (30–38cm)
SPREAD	18–24in (45–60cm)
HABIT	Upright bush
HARDINESS	Half hardy
FLOWERING	Summer to first frost

P

'Pink Rain'

CASCADES OF TWO-TONE PINK FLOWERS hang from the trailing stems of 'Pink Rain'. The effect is heightened by the stamens and pistil that dangle well below the hem of the corolla. A good-natured plant that is easy to grow, you can encourage it to thicken up by pinching back stems in spring and early summer. Use it as the principal plant in a mixed hanging basket with small-leaved ivies, and position it in light shade to preserve its delicate colors.

PLANT PROFILE	
HEIGHT 9–12in (23–30cm)	
SPREAD 15–18in (38–45cm)	
HABIT Trailing, self-branching	
HARDINESS Half hardy	
FLOWERING Summer to first frost	

'Pixie'

'PIXIE' PROVIDES A DOUBLE BLAST OF COLOR. As if yellow-green foliage with crimson veining wasn't bright enough, this cultivar also produces masses of small, vivid red and rosy mauve flowers. You may find it offered ready-trained as a small standard, but it is also highly rated as a permanent low hedge. Having proved itself hardy in many areas, it may be safe to leave outside all winter with a covering of shredded bark.

P

PLANT PROFILE

HEIGHT 3ft (1m)

SPREAD 4ft (1.2m)

HABIT Upright bush, self-branching

HARDINESS Fully hardy

FLOWERING Summer

P

'Plenty'

PLENTY IS AN UNDERSTATEMENT because it produces rose and violet flowers in great profusion. The plant gets top grades, too, for its shapeliness, since it is very bushy, upright, and short-jointed. Although it is naturally branched, it responds well to frequent pinching and is easy to train to most shapes, except trailing. It grows exceptionally well in a conservatory or glasshouse and also makes a good summer bedder. In mild areas, 'Plenty' may survive winter outdoors if given a thick covering of shredded bark.

PLANT PROFILE

HEIGHT 18–24in (45–60cm)

SPREAD 15–18in (38–45cm)

HABIT Upright bush, self-branching

HARDINESS Half hardy

FLOWERING Summer to first frost

'Powder Puff'

P

A PERFECT NAME for such a soft-colored double fuchsia.
The tube and strongly recurved sepals are rose pink with
an apple blossom pink corolla. A dark background will set
them off to perfection. The lax, trailing growth makes it an
extremely useful plant for hanging baskets. Rather confusingly,
this free-flowering American cultivar, introduced in 1953,
shares the same name as a more recent, but vastly different,
British fuchsia that is a very compact, low-growing bush.

PLANT PROFILE

HEIGHT 9–12in (22–30cm)

SPREAD 15–18in (38–45cm)

HABIT Trailing, self-branching

HARDINESS Half hardy

FLOWERING Summer to first frost

P

'President George Bartlett'

A STRIKING, UPRIGHT FUCHSIA, 'President George Bartlett' (named after the distinguished British fuchsia expert) has deep red tubes and sepals with dark violet corollas aging to ruby red. The leaves are a glossy, dark green. It will liven up any display, especially when the flower supply of other plants starts to peter out in late summer. Introduced at the end of the 20th century, this imposing cultivar is worth tracking down through a specialist nursery. In some areas it can be safely left outdoors over the winter.

PLANT PROFILE	
HEIGHT 18in (45cm)	
SPREAD 18–24in (45–60cm)	
HABIT Upright bush	
HARDINESS Borderline frost hardy	
FLOWERING Summer	

'President Leo Boullemier'

P

THIS STUNNING FUCHSIA was named in honor of a former president of the British Fuchsia Society. The flowers have long, upswept white sepals and a bell-shaped, magenta-blue corolla that matures to pink. The effect is stunning, especially because they are produced in such great numbers. 'President Leo Boullemier' deserves a prominent place on the patio or in a courtyard garden in a grand ornamental pot.

PLANT PROFILE	
HEIGHT 15in (38cm)	
SPREAD 18–24in (45–60cm)	
HABIT Upright bush	
HARDINESS Half hardy	
FLOWERING Summer to first frost	

P

'President Margaret Slater'

ANOTHER EXQUISITE FUCHSIA named after a past president
of the British Fuchsia Society. Vigorous, trailing stems heavy
with flowers make it a superb subject for a hanging basket,
although it is also easily trained as a standard. Subtle shifts in
color give the single flowers an added dimension. The long,
thin tube is clear white, while the slightly twisted, white sepals
are gently flushed with pink. The pink darkens again when it
reaches the corolla, taking on strong mauve tones overlaid
with salmon.

PLANT PROFILE

HEIGHT 12–18in (30–45cm)

SPREAD 18–30in (45–75cm)

HABIT Trailing

HARDINESS Half hardy

FLOWERING Summer to first frost

'Preston Guild'

P

WITH THEIR SWEPT-BACK SEPALS and long, dangling stamens and pistil, the flowers of 'Preston Guild' look like ornamental lanterns. They are produced in such numbers that the upright stems look as though they have been hung with strings of lights. Such stunning looks more than compensate for its shorter-than-average flowering season and a habit of dropping its blooms. It makes a superb summer bedding plant, but place it in light shade to protect the petal colors—bright sun will turn the sepals pink.

PLANT PROFILE	
HEIGHT 3ft (1m)	
SPREAD 18–24in (45–60cm)	
HABIT Upright bush	
HARDINESS Frost hardy	
FLOWERING Summer to first frost	

P *procumbens*

MORE OF A CURIOSITY THAN A BEAUTY, in its native habitat of New Zealand this species fuchsia is found growing on the sandy dunes beside the sea, where its trailing stems of heart-shaped leaves can reach over 20ft (6m). The rather unprepossessing flowers are small but freely produced, with green-yellow tubes and green-purple sepals. Unusually, there is no corolla and the stamens are tipped with bright blue pollen. The main event, though, is the green seed pods which, if left to mature, turn purple and swell to plum size. Grow it in a hanging basket or to trail over a rock wall or sunny slope.

PLANT PROFILE

HEIGHT 4–6in (10–15cm)

SPREAD 3–4ft (1–1.2m)

HABIT Trailing

HARDINESS Z9–11 H12–9

FLOWERING Summer to autumn

'Prosperity'

P

VIGOROUS AND HARDY, 'Prosperity' is a multipurpose cultivar
that is hardy in many areas, and can be left outside year-round
if given a thick winter mulch of shredded bark. Extremely
free-flowering, it is a must for an old-fashioned cottage garden
plan, as a bedding plant or a low hedge. Its strong, upright
stems also respond well to training, and it makes a superb
standard. Unusually, the leaves, which are dark green, glossy,
and strongly serrated, are grouped in threes at most leaf joints.

PLANT PROFILE	
HEIGHT 24in (60cm)	
SPREAD 24in (60cm)	
HABIT Upright bush	
HARDINESS Fully hardy	
FLOWERING Summer	

P

'Purperklokje'

A HIGHLY UNUSUAL DUTCH FUCHSIA that was introduced in
the late 1980s. It has very small, slender flowers with intense
coloration—pinkish eggplant on the tubes and sepals, and
a very fashionable dark eggplant on the corollas. The flowers
are nicely displayed and stand out well from the low, bushy
growth. Don't crowd it out with other plants—it is much too
good for that; give it a solo spot in an ornamental pot.

PLANT PROFILE	
HEIGHT 24–30in (60–75cm)	
SPREAD 15–18in (38–45cm)	
HABIT Upright bush	
HARDINESS Half hardy	
FLOWERING Summer to first frost	

'Quasar'

WITH ITS MASSIVE, DOUBLE FLOWERS, 'Quasar' guarantees a magnificent show for a hanging basket or pot. To display its white and purple flowers to their full potential, it must be allowed to trail its long stems over the edge of the container. If grown in a container, stand it on top of a wall or pillar, since it would be a crime to allow its flowers to trail on the ground. For the best petal color, grow it in shade.

PLANT PROFILE
HEIGHT 12–15in (30–38cm)
SPREAD 18–24in (45–60cm)
HABIT Trailing
HARDINESS Half hardy
FLOWERING Summer to first frost

Q | 'Queen Mary'

AN INTROSPECTIVE FUCHSIA that is perfectly suited to informal
cottage-garden-style planting. The pale pink tube and sepals
crown a rose corolla that matures to deep mauve. Some
growers have noted that its performance as a bedding plant
can be a little disappointing, but it is quite happy in an
ornamental planter or when trained as a regal standard.
A backdrop of dark-colored bark, decking, or pebbles will
highlight the subtle coloring. If grown outdoors instead of
under glass, this cultivar may be late to flower.

PLANT PROFILE

HEIGHT 15–18in (38–45cm)

SPREAD 15–18in (38–45cm)

HABIT Upright bush

HARDINESS Half hardy

FLOWERING Summer to first frost

'R.A.F.'

R

LIKE TINY PARACHUTISTS POISED TO JUMP, masses of billowing, double blooms in strong red and rose pink hang from the stems of 'R.A.F.' The growth is sufficiently lax to make it a suitable fuchsia for a hanging basket, although with careful staking and pinching out, it can be coerced to grow as an upright bush. Despite its military name, this fuchsia has an informal air that's in keeping with cottage gardens.

PLANT PROFILE	
HEIGHT 12–15in (30–38cm)	
SPREAD 12–15in (30–38cm)	
HABIT Trailing or lax bush, self-branching	
HARDINESS Half hardy	
FLOWERING Summer to first frost	

R | 'Ravensbarrow'

SMART AND SOPHISTICATED, the flowers of 'Ravensbarrow' echo the rich, purple–black corolla of the black fuchsia ('Black Prince'), its parent plant. They are small but freely produced, and are perfectly in scale with the equally dainty, dark green foliage. It is highly prized as a well-proportioned miniature standard. The strong colors have plenty of punch and will jump-start any planting plan that looks jaded and lackluster.

PLANT PROFILE

HEIGHT 18–24in (45–60cm)

SPREAD 24–36in (60–90cm)

HABIT Upright bush

HARDINESS Half hardy

FLOWERING Summer to first frost

'Red Shadows'

A DUAL-PURPOSE FUCHSIA that looks equally good in pots or trailing out of hanging baskets. Each flower is an attractive mix of crimson tube and sepals, with a burgundy corolla that goes through several color changes before maturing to ruby red. Not surprisingly, these curiously ruffled blooms are very popular with flower arrangers. The growth habit of 'Red Shadows' is relaxed, loose, and bushy, making it perfect for summer bedding in any informal display, especially where the colors need a boost.

PLANT PROFILE
HEIGHT 18–24in (45–60cm)
SPREAD 15–18in (38–45cm)
HABIT Trailing or lax bush
HARDINESS Half hardy
FLOWERING Summer to first frost

R 'Red Spider'

A SUITABLE, IF BIZARRE, NAME for a fuchsia with long, slender, dangling flowers that are a glorious combination of crimson and deep rose pink. As they mature, the sepals also have an interesting habit of curving back on themselves. It is an extremely vigorous, free-flowering, and thoroughly reliable fuchsia that responds well to early pinching. With a little training, it will make a nicely shaped basket plant.

PLANT PROFILE

HEIGHT 6–12in (15–30cm)

SPREAD 12–24in (30–60cm)

HABIT Trailing, self-branching

HARDINESS Z9–11 H12–9

FLOWERING Summer to first frost

'Riccartonii'

R

THE MOST POPULAR HARDY FUCHSIA, 'Riccartonii' is often
found growing as a tall hedge in western England and in
Ireland, where the high rainfall and humidity suit it well.
Strong, upright stems bear dark green, bronzy leaves together
with masses of dangling scarlet and dark purple flowers that
have been given the appropriate nickname of lady's eardrops.
If top growth is killed by frost, it will reshoot from the base in
spring. You may find this listed as *F. magellanica* 'Riccartonii'
or *F. magellanica* var. *riccartonii*.

PLANT PROFILE	
HEIGHT 6–10ft (2–3m)	
SPREAD 3–6ft (1–2m)	
HABIT Upright bush	
HARDINESS Z8–10 H10–8	
FLOWERING Summer to autumn	

R

'Ridestar'

WITH FLOWERS IN A CLASSIC COLOR combination of red and deep lilac, 'Ridestar' is upright and bushy, and guarantees a good show for the summer border. For a loud display, plant it beside other strong reds, such as *Lobelia* 'Queen Victoria', *Canna* 'King Humbert', and *Salvia elegans*. It will also stand out well against jazzy yellow annuals. For a more harmonious planting, mix it with a palette of blues and violets.

PLANT PROFILE

HEIGHT 15–18in (38–45cm)

SPREAD 15–18in (38–45cm))

HABIT Upright bush, self-branching

HARDINESS Half hardy

FLOWERING Summer to first frost

'Ringwood Market'

R

A PASTEL COLOR SCHEME of soft rose and powder blue makes an elegant change from more strident cultivars. With age, the blue corolla gently fades to an equally soft lilac. The semidouble flowers are a good size, nicely compact, and freely produced, and will act as a calming influence in a busy border packed with reds, oranges, and yellows.

PLANT PROFILE	
HEIGHT 12–15in (30–38cm)	
SPREAD 12–15in (30–38cm)	
HABIT Upright bush	
HARDINESS Half hardy	
FLOWERING Summer to first frost	

R 'Rocket Fire'

A SLIGHTLY AMBITIOUS NAME for a fuchsia that's just 24in (60cm) high, but it is covered with beautiful magenta, rose, and purple flowers and has rich green foliage. These qualities make it an exceptional container plant with plenty of presence. Use it to draw attention to important garden features, to signal the start of a path, frame doorways, or to encircle an ornamental pond with a ring of bright color.

PLANT PROFILE

HEIGHT 18–24in (45–60cm)

SPREAD 15–18in (38–45cm)

HABIT Upright bush or trailing

HARDINESS Half hardy

FLOWERING Summer to first frost

'Rose Fantasia'

R

A FUCHSIA WITH A DIFFERENCE, 'Rose Fantasia' has beautifully colored flowers that are not uniformly pendulous—in fact, they often point upward instead of hanging down. Plant it separately from other more conventional fuchsias or the effect will be diluted. Incredibly bushy and producing a mass of blooms, it makes a fabulous summer bedder or container plant.

PLANT PROFILE

HEIGHT 18–24in (45–60cm)

SPREAD 15–18in (38–45cm)

HABIT Upright bush, self-branching

HARDINESS Z9–11 H12–9

FLOWERING Summer to first frost

R | 'Rose of Castile'

AN ELEGANT FUCHSIA WITH SUBTLE COLORING that combines a blend of soft rose pinks and purple flushed with rose. Each petal in the corolla carries a white central streak. Although the flowers are small and single, they put on a wonderful show, appearing in great numbers over a long period throughout summer. The stiff, vigorous stems and bushy growth make 'Rose of Castile' ideal for pots or for training as a standard.

PLANT PROFILE

HEIGHT 18in (45cm)

SPREAD 15–18in (38–45cm)

HABIT Upright bush, self-branching

HARDINESS Z9–11 H12–9

FLOWERING Summer to first frost

'Rose of Castile Improved'

R

THE FIRST 'ROSE OF CASTILE' appeared in 1855 and the "Improved" version 16 years later. The latter is very different from its predecessor but is not really a great improvement on it, except that it is on a noticeably grander scale, with larger pink and violet purple flowers. 'Rose of Castile Improved' makes a strong-growing summer bedding plant or a good feature for a mixed container.

PLANT PROFILE	
HEIGHT 24–30in (60–75cm)	
SPREAD 18–24in (45–60cm)	
HABIT Upright bush	
HARDINESS Frost hardy	
FLOWERING Summer to first frost	

R 'Rose of Denmark'

THE MEDIUM-SIZED, LOOSE-PETALED full flowers of 'Rose of Denmark' are delicately colored and perfect if you have a passion for pink. Mostly single, you may get some semidoubles thrown in as a treat. The sepals are noticeably broader than usual and upswept. Grow 'Rose of Denmark' in a border or train it as a standard—either way, it produces bushy growth and an excellent show of pastel-colored flowers.

PLANT PROFILE	
HEIGHT	24in (60cm)
SPREAD	36in (90cm)
HABIT	Lax bush
HARDINESS	Borderline hardy
FLOWERING	Summer to first frost

'Royal Mosaic'

R

THE "MOSAIC" PART OF THE NAME rightly denotes the slightly varying colors of the corolla. They initially have a violet-blue coloration that gradually becomes rose-tinted and contrasts well with the cream and pink marbling on the sepals. The warm tones are repeated on the red stems and the veining on the leaves. Grow it in hanging baskets where the trailing stems can dangle down.

PLANT PROFILE	
HEIGHT 9–12in (23–30cm)	
SPREAD 15–18in (38–45cm)	
HABIT Trailing	
HARDINESS Half hardy	
FLOWERING Summer to first frost	

R | 'Royal Velvet'

A SPECTACULAR FUCHSIA with large, double flowers in two
equally strong colors—crimson and deep purple. The ruffled
petals of the corolla are so tightly packed that it looks like a
frilly petticoat. As the flower ages, the petals open out to reveal
a dash of crimson at their base. Help the plant put its efforts
into bushing out rather than gaining height by regularly
pinching out new shoots. You can also boost the production of
flower buds by keeping it slightly potbound. If using 'Royal
Velvet' as bedding, don't plant it in bright sun or the petals
will fade. It also makes a good standard.

PLANT PROFILE

HEIGHT 18–30in (45–75cm)

SPREAD 12–24in (30–60cm)

HABIT Upright bush,
self-branching

HARDINESS Z9–11 H12–9

FLOWERING Summer to first frost

'Rufus'

R

SOMETIMES CALLED 'RUFUS THE RED', this is an impressive one-color fuchsia that is awash with single, medium-sized, bright red flowers over a long period. Growth is naturally fast, upright, and bushy, and it will make a shapely, early flowering hedge or bush for the border. In winter, protect it from severe frost with a thick covering of shredded bark. 'Rufus' can also be grown as a robust standard, gaining a good deal of height in just one year.

PLANT PROFILE

HEIGHT 18–30in (45–75cm)

SPREAD 12–24in (30–60cm)

HABIT Upright bush

HARDINESS Z9–11 H12–9

FLOWERING Summer to autumn

R | 'Ruth'

GETTING OFF TO AN EARLY START, 'Ruth' is an all-red fuchsia that will reliably perform all summer. It is worth considering if your first-choice red is not available, since it is an easy one to grow and care for. Make the most of its red flowers in late summer by positioning it close to the beige seedheads and stems of ornamental grasses. Another happy coupling is beneath the climbing *Clematis* 'Bill MacKenzie', which has yellow flowers and silvery seedheads.

PLANT PROFILE	
HEIGHT 24in (60cm)	
SPREAD 36in (90cm)	
HABIT Upright bush	
HARDINESS Fully hardy	
FLOWERING Summer	

'Santa Monica'

'SANTA MONICA' COMBINES PALE RED on the tube and sepals with light pink on the corolla. In the open garden, its delicate, introspective tones create a calm oasis among bright, brash summer bedding, and it is the perfect choice for a pot on a dark wood deck, where its double flowers will stand out well.

PLANT PROFILE

HEIGHT 24in (60cm)

SPREAD 18in (45cm)

HABIT Upright bush

HARDINESS Half hardy

FLOWERING Summer to first frost

S

'Sarah Jane'

SMALL AND COMPACT THE FLOWERS MAY BE, but they are
produced in such numbers that the effect is quite special. This
cultivar's blend of soft red and lilac makes it a good mixer for
the summer border or a large patio container. If you live in a
mild area, you could take a chance and leave this fuchsia
outside for the winter, but give it a fighting chance by covering
the crown with a thick layer of shredded bark.

PLANT PROFILE

HEIGHT 24in (60cm)

SPREAD 30in (75cm)

HABIT Upright, spreading bush

HARDINESS Half hardy

FLOWERING Summer to first frost

'Saturnus'

S

SMALL BUT SASSY, 'Saturnus' is deserving of a place right at the front of any display, where it will proceed to put on a good show of color all summer long. The red sepals, which give the single flowers a distinctive look, hover like wings over each red-veined, purple corolla. Frame the plant with a couple of pastel-colored fuchsias, or grow it in a pot to complement a favorite garden feature.

PLANT PROFILE		
HEIGHT 12–15in (30–38cm)		
SPREAD 15–18in (38–45cm)		
HABIT Upright bush		
HARDINESS Half hardy		
FLOWERING Summer to first frost		

S | 'Scarcity'

BOLD AND BRASH, use scarlet and purple 'Scarcity' as a focal
point among pastel-colored fuchsias and summer annuals.
A very early and prolific flowerer, by the end of June it will be
a mass of color. It is hardy in some areas and can be left safely
in the border over winter if given a covering of shredded
bark. Raised by James Lye in 1869, this wonderful cultivar is
well worth tracking down from a specialist nursery.

PLANT PROFILE

HEIGHT 18in (45cm)

SPREAD 18in (45cm)

HABIT Upright bush

HARDINESS Fully hardy

FLOWERING Summer

'Sealand Prince'

S

UPRIGHT AND BUSHY, when planted in a container 'Sealand Prince' makes a perfect filler plant for any awkward gaps in the early summer garden. Simply maneuver it into position and let its cheerful mix of light red and violet purple single flowers brighten up a dull area. In mild areas it can be left outside over winter in the border, but if a heavy frost is forecast, protect the crown with a thick layer of shredded bark.

PLANT PROFILE	
HEIGHT	24–30in (60–75cm)
SPREAD	15–18in (38–45cm)
HABIT	Upright bush
HARDINESS	Frost hardy
FLOWERING	Summer

S

'Shelford'

IN ITS FIRST SEASON 'Shelford' is guaranteed to make a prize-winning fuchsia, producing plenty of blooms and vigorous, bushy growth. The subtle combination of baby pink and white doesn't jump out at you, but it is clearly a beautifully colored plant that deserves attention. Choose a spot in light shade to give extra warmth to the pink and a lift to the white. Definitely worth a place in anyone's collection, use 'Shelford' in containers or as a good mixer in the summer border.

PLANT PROFILE

HEIGHT 15–18in (38–45cm)

SPREAD 15–18in (38–45cm)

HABIT Upright bush

HARDINESS Z9–11 H12–9

FLOWERING Summer to first frost

'Sleigh Bells'

S

THE COROLLA OF THIS ALL-WHITE FUCHSIA forms a perfect
bell shape, and the sepals are shapely too, slowly curling over
the tube as the single flower matures. Growth is bushy and
upright, although by nipping out the growing tips in spring
and early summer, you will encourage more shoots to grow
from the base of the plant. Like other white fuchsias, it is
susceptible to botrytis. To prevent it, avoid overwatering and
ensure that the plant is well ventilated.

PLANT PROFILE	
HEIGHT 15–18in (38–45cm)	
SPREAD 12–15in (30–38cm)	
HABIT Upright bush	
HARDINESS Half hardy	
FLOWERING Summer to first frost	

S | 'Snow Burner'

AN UNUSUAL NAME FOR AN UNUSUAL FUCHSIA, 'Snow Burner' is grown for its very large flowers that are a combination of a fiery red tube and sepals, and an ice white corolla with red veining. Planted in the summer border or in containers, its stems will need staking to counter a natural lax tendency and to support the weight of the heavy blooms. It can also be grown in a hanging basket and, although the stems will need weighing down in the early stages of training to encourage them to trail, the final effect is well worth the effort.

PLANT PROFILE

HEIGHT 12–15in (30–38cm)

SPREAD 18–24in (45–60cm)

HABIT Lax bush

HARDINESS Half hardy

FLOWERING Summer to first frost

'Snowcap'

BRIGHT, BRASH, AND FLASHY, 'Snowcap' produces scores of red and white flowers against a perfect backdrop of small, dark green leaves. Easy to grow and trouble-free, this fuchsia is a good cultivar to cut your teeth on. Train it as a standard or, for a bushier profile, keep pinching it back to thicken up the stems around the base of the plant. In mild areas it can stay outside in the border over winter—even if growth is cut back by frost, it will reshoot from the base in spring. Regarded as one of the most free-flowering cultivars available, it copes with full sun but prefers semishade.

PLANT PROFILE	
HEIGHT	24–30in (60–75cm)
SPREAD	24–30in (60–75cm)
HABIT	Upright, self-branching
HARDINESS	Z9–11 H12–9
FLOWERING	Summer to autumn

S | 'Snowfire'

A USEFUL, MULTIPURPOSE FUCHSIA, 'Snowfire' can be grown as a bushy pot plant or trained as a standard. The double flowers are stunning, especially the petals of the corolla, which consist of a rose pink petticoat under a frilly skirt of pink and white. Before they open, the buds are also streaked with rose pink. 'Snowfire' is a naturally bushy plant but, since you can never have too much of a good thing, many growers like to pinch out the stem tips in spring and early summer to encourage thicker growth near the base of the plant.

PLANT PROFILE

HEIGHT 18–24in (45–60cm)

SPREAD 15–18in (38–45cm)

HABIT Upright bush

HARDINESS Half hardy

FLOWERING Summer to first frost

'Son of Thumb'

SHORT, BUSHY, AND COMPACT, this fuchsia is just like its parent plant, 'Tom Thumb'. 'Son of Thumb' also flowers over a long period, producing masses of small, single blooms in rich shades of cherry red and lilac. A fantastic dwarf fuchsia for the front of a border, it is reasonably hardy and will survive outdoors over winter in mild areas (cover the crown with a thick layer of shredded bark). Use it to brighten up window boxes, containers, and gravel gardens.

S

PLANT PROFILE

HEIGHT 12–18in (30–45cm)

SPREAD 12–18in (30–45cm)

HABIT Dwarf, upright bush self-branching

HARDINESS Borderline frost hardy

FLOWERING Summer to autumn

S

'South Gate'

EXCEPTIONALLY FULL AND FRILLY, the large double flowers of 'South Gate' look like a cheerleader's pom-poms, and it should come as no surprise to learn that it was first introduced in the US in the 1950s. The blooms are produced in huge numbers and put on quite a show. Easy to grow and train, the stems are upright but rather lax, which means it will grow as a loose bush, or it can be enticed to trail from a hanging basket. With early training, it also makes a strong standard and is good for brightening up any summer garden.

PLANT PROFILE

HEIGHT	18–24in (45–60cm)
SPREAD	18–24in (45–60cm)
HABIT	Lax bush
HARDINESS	Half hardy
FLOWERING	Summer to first frost

'Space Shuttle'

JUSTIFIABLY HIGHLY RATED, 'Space Shuttle' has distinctive, very beautiful flowers and a low, sprawling habit. The long tube and green-tipped sepals are soft red, while the corolla is pale yellow with an orange base, aging to light orange. Flowers appear throughout the year, but strong summer sun and heat ruin the yellow tones, so the blooms are usually at their best in winter and spring. With encouragement, the lax stems make a good hanging basket plant, while regular pinching—and the occasional supporting cane—will help the plant to form a neat, bushy shape.

S

PLANT PROFILE

HEIGHT 3–6in (8–15cm)

SPREAD 9–12in (23–30cm)

HABIT Lax, upright bush or stiff trailer

HARDINESS Half hardy

FLOWERING All year

S

'Spion Kop'

SUBTLE COLORS INFUSE THE PETALS of this low-growing fuchsia. The white, double corolla is attractively marked with rose red veining, while a row of petaloids (small petals) tucked under the sepals give the flower a delicate frilliness. Although the vigorous, upright stems are naturally bushy, this fuchsia responds well to frequent pinching and makes a superb, easy-to-grow container plant. Raised in Great Britain in 1973, the name 'Spion Kop' derives from a 1900 battle site in the South African War (1899–1902).

PLANT PROFILE

HEIGHT 12–15in (30–38cm)

SPREAD 15–18in (38–45cm)

HABIT Upright bush

HARDINESS Half hardy

FLOWERING Summer to first frost

splendens

S

A SPECIES FUCHSIA, *F. splendens* is from the warm, moist forests of the eastern coast of Central America, from Mexico to Costa Rica, where it can reach up to 8ft (2.5m). Rest assured that even when grown in a conservatory or warm greenhouse, it will reach only half that size. Although naturally shrubby, when grown in a container it takes on a very bushy shape. A restricted root run will increase flower production. The flowers, which have a flattened tube, are followed by sweet-sour tasting berries that ripen to purple-green. Highly rated by experts, *F. splendens* is well worth seeking out.

PLANT PROFILE

HEIGHT 24–30in (60–75cm)

SPREAD 24in (60cm)

HABIT Upright bush

HARDINESS Z9–11 H12–9

FLOWERING Summer

S

'Stella Ann'

BEAUTIFUL 'STELLA ANN' carries the distinctive long tube of
a Triphylla-type fuchsia, although it is thicker and more
tapering than others in this group. The poppy red and coral
flowers hang in numerous dangling clusters, standing out well
against the large, rich green leaves with their dark purple veins
and red undersides. Such vigorous, colorful growth gives this
fuchsia plenty of impact, and it makes a strong focal point in
a display of potted plants.

PLANT PROFILE

HEIGHT 15–18in (38–45cm)

SPREAD 12–15in (30–38cm)

HABIT Upright bush,
self-branching

HARDINESS Frost tender

FLOWERING Summer

'Strawberry Delight'

S

A FLAMBOYANT CHOICE FOR A HANGING BASKET, 'Strawberry Delight' has a crimson tube and sepals and a white corolla infused with strawberry ripples. The foliage has a distinctive bronze patina. It is an attractive plant for a patio pot or hanging basket because its spreading stems, while lax and naturally trailing, have enough body in them to give a good weeping shape.

PLANT PROFILE	
HEIGHT	15–18in (38–45cm)
SPREAD	12–15in (30–38cm)
HABIT	Trailing
HARDINESS	Z9–11 H12–9
FLOWERING	Summer to first frost

S | 'String of Pearls'

THE NAME SAYS IT ALL—the pale pink and lilac semidouble blooms appear in lengths, just like strings of pearls, over the long, arching stems. It is an exceptionally prolific flowerer and, while growth is strong and relatively bushy, pinching out the growing tips in early summer will encourage more stems to shoot from the base. Although it makes a good multipurpose bush, it is not especially easy to train to shape; however, it can sometimes be bought ready-trained as a standard. For the best flower color, plant 'String of Pearls' in a shady spot.

PLANT PROFILE

HEIGHT 18–24in (45–60cm)

SPREAD 18–24in (45–60cm)

HABIT Upright bush

HARDINESS Half hardy

FLOWERING Summer to first frost

'Sunset Boulevard'

S

UNBELIEVABLY RICH, VELVETY COLORS in shades of purple, burgundy, red, and pink make this trailing fuchsia a fabulous choice for a hanging basket. Keep it out of strong, direct sunlight to stop the petals from fading. With early pinching you will encourage the stems to branch and, in a surprisingly short space of time, make a lovely rounded shape.

PLANT PROFILE	
HEIGHT	6–10in (15–25cm)
SPREAD	10in (25cm)
HABIT	Lax, trailing
HARDINESS	Frost hardy
FLOWERING	Summer

S

'Superstar'

THE NAME MAY BE A SLIGHT EXAGGERATION but 'Superstar' does have plenty of presence. Its medium-sized, single blooms are plentiful and colorful. Use it to fill gaps in the front of a border, where it will settle in comfortably among pastels, or next to loud red tones that need the sting taken out of them. Its upright, dense growth habit makes it easy to train, either as a bush or as a standard.

PLANT PROFILE

HEIGHT 15–18in (38–45cm)

SPREAD 15–18in (38–45cm)

HABIT Upright bush

HARDINESS Half hardy

FLOWERING Summer to first frost

'Susan Green'

S

A BEAUTIFUL FUCHSIA THAT'S EASY TO TRAIN, either as a weeping standard or as a trailing plant for a hanging basket. Its strong, even stems respond well to pinching out in spring and early summer, and seem to thicken up almost overnight. 'Susan Green' is a good choice when building up a collection of fuchsias, since the pink, bell-shaped flowers are an especially useful addition to pastel color schemes.

PLANT PROFILE	
HEIGHT 12–15in (30–38cm)	
SPREAD 18in (45cm)	
HABIT Trailing, self-branching	
HARDINESS Half hardy	
FLOWERING Summer to first frost	

S | 'Susan Travis'

QUIET PASTEL PINKS make 'Susan Travis' a good mixer in the summer border, where its calming influence is invaluable for cooling down overheated color schemes. The flowers, which are unusually subtle for a hardy fuchsia, are freely produced on strong, spreading stems. When placing it in the garden, remember that maximum height is achieved a couple of years before maximum spread. The plant is hardy enough to be left outside over winter in mild regions, as long as the crown is covered with a thick layer of shredded bark before temperatures fall below freezing.

PLANT PROFILE

HEIGHT 24in (60cm)

SPREAD 18in (45cm)

HABIT Upright bush

HARDINESS Fully hardy

FLOWERING Summer

'Swingtime'

BIG AND SHOWY, the upper parts of the flower are a rich red while the sparkling white petals of the double corolla look like a billowing skirt. The long, lax stems (not quite trailing, but horizontal when weighed down by the large flowers) make it a fine choice for a hanging basket. It responds particularly well to frequent pinching out and, with careful training, it will also make a stately standard.

PLANT PROFILE

HEIGHT 12–24in (30–60cm)

SPREAD 18–30in (45–75cm)

HABIT Trailing or lax upright bush, self-branching

HARDINESS Z9–11 H12–9

FLOWERING Summer to first frost

T | 'Taddle'

A STRONG-GROWING FUCHSIA, 'Taddle' has a naturally upright, bushy habit that makes it a good feature plant for a patio planter. The compact blooms are freely produced and are a lovely combination of pastel shades: deep rose pink on the sepals—which, incidentally, sweep back almost to the vertical, practically hiding the deep rose tube—and a waxy white single corolla that carries the faintest pink veining. The foliage is a suitably soft light green.

PLANT PROFILE

HEIGHT 18–24in (45–60cm)

SPREAD 12–18in (30–45cm)

HABIT Upright bush

HARDINESS Half hardy

FLOWERING Summer to first frost

'Tennessee Waltz'

T

THE FREE-AND-EASY DISPLAY of pink and lilac flowers is exactly what you need in an informal cottage garden. Growth is vigorous and won't let you down, and there is an abundance of flowers—once buds start to open, the blooms will keep coming right up to the first frost. It is a very easy cultivar to grow, and if you've never tried training a bush or standard, it's a good beginner's plant, producing a nice bushy shape after its first session of pinch-training. Within six months you can expect a rooted cutting to make a good-sized plant.

PLANT PROFILE	
HEIGHT 24in (60cm)	
SPREAD 18–24in (45–60cm)	
HABIT Upright bush	
HARDINESS Z8–10	
FLOWERING Summer to first frost	

T

'Tequila Sunrise'

A SUPERLATIVE BASKET FUCHSIA, 'Tequila Sunrise' produces huge numbers of small single flowers in a stunning blend of salmon and dark pink. As the flowers age, the sepals lift to the horizontal to reveal light pink markings on the base of the corolla petals. It is a very vigorous cultivar that will quickly make a lovely, rounded basket plant, especially if you pinch the stems immediately after planting. The foliage is noted for its robustness and withstands high temperatures. Impress visitors by hanging a pair of baskets on either side of the front door.

PLANT PROFILE

HEIGHT 6–10in (15–25cm)

SPREAD 10in (25cm)

HABIT Trailing

HARDINESS Frost hardy

FLOWERING Summer

'Texas Longhorn'

T

ITS CLAIM TO FAME is that each flower has very wide sepals, sometimes 9in (23cm) from "wing" to "wing," though the rest of the flower is not in proportion because the corollas are quite small. The flowers are red on the tube and sepals, while the corolla is white. Growth is lax, which is why it is grown as a trailer for hanging baskets, but you will have to keep nipping out the growing stems in spring and early summer to force out more flowering stems lower down. Note that 'Texas Longhorn' is infamous for its relative lack of flowers.

PLANT PROFILE		
HEIGHT 9–12in (23–30cm)		
SPREAD 18–24in (45–60cm)		
HABIT Trailing		
HARDINESS Z9–11 H12–9		
FLOWERING Summer to first frost		

T | 'Thalia'

DISTINGUISHED BY ITS LONG, THIN, FLAME RED flowers, this early-20th-century German fuchsia has remained incredibly popular since its introduction. It is unmistakably a Triphylla-type fuchsia, with its pointed flowers appearing in huge numbers over a long season—from a distance, and with the late afternoon sun on it, the bush can look as though it's on fire. The olive green foliage is equally colorful, with magenta veining and purple undersides. The vigorous, upright growth can be made much bushier by nipping out the growing tips when young.

PLANT PROFILE

HEIGHT	18–36in (45–90cm)
SPREAD	18–36in (45–90cm)
HABIT	Upright bush
HARDINESS	Z9–11 H12–9
FLOWERING	Summer to autumn

'Thamar'

RARELY MENTIONED IN GARDENING BOOKS, 'Thamar' is an exquisite pastel-colored bushy fuchsia with white upper sections, running into a soft, gentle, bluish white on the corolla. The flowers are held upward and outward on short, erect stems at each leaf joint. Grow it in a large container in dappled light so that the blue tones appear slightly stronger.

T

PLANT PROFILE

HEIGHT 18–24in (45–60cm)

SPREAD 18–24in (45–60cm)

HABIT Upright bush

HARDINESS Half hardy

FLOWERING Summer to first frost

T | 'The Doctor'

AS SUMMER GETS UNDERWAY, the branches of 'The Doctor' will start to bend under the weight of a profusion of pink and pale red flowers. In terms of habit, it's an "in-betweener"—rather too lax for an upright bush and noticeably stiffer than most trailers (but that's not to say it can't be trained as a basket plant). Perhaps the best place for it would be in a large terracotta pot among a massed display of fuchsias, where each plant can tumble into its neighbor, creating a huge block of summer color. It also makes a surprisingly good standard.

PLANT PROFILE

HEIGHT	12–15in (30–38cm)
SPREAD	24in (60cm)
HABIT	Trailing
HARDINESS	Half hardy
FLOWERING	Summer to first frost

thymifolia

T

BUY *F. THYMIFOLIA* when the flowers are just opening and you will probably think that it is going to be all white. In fact, the tube reddens with age and the corolla changes to a rosy purple, but these fluctuating colors give the plant an added dimension. The growth habit of this species fuchsia is upright and very bushy, with the slenderest of wiry stems—support from canes wouldn't hurt. Incidentally, you can boost flowering by restricting the root run on pot-grown plants. If you're looking for something a little different, *F. thymifolia* is worth tracking down from a specialist nursery.

PLANT PROFILE
HEIGHT 18–24in (45–60cm)
SPREAD 15–18in (38–45cm)
HABIT Upright bush
HARDINESS Z9–11 H12–9
FLOWERING Summer

T | 'Tillingbourne'

THIS COLORFUL CULTIVAR makes a welcome addition to
a bed of fuchsias. The strong growth makes a neat and tidy
upright bush with mid-green foliage that always looks healthy.
The double flowers, made up of pink sepals and a purple
corolla with a pink base, are large for a hardy fuchsia and very
striking. In warm, sheltered areas it will survive winter if given
a protective covering of shredded bark to keep out the worst
of the weather.

PLANT PROFILE	
HEIGHT	18in (45cm)
SPREAD	24in (60cm)
HABIT	Upright bush
HARDINESS	Borderline hardy
FLOWERING	Summer to first frost

'Tinker Bell'

T

NEAT, PETITE 'TINKER BELL' needs a spot right at the front
of a display, since everything about it is on a diminutive scale.
Far from being shy, however, this charming fuchsia's arching
stems are packed with vibrant red and white bell-shaped
flowers. Given a protective covering of shredded bark in
winter, it is tough enough to stay outside all year in milder
regions. 'Tinker Bell' makes a perfect edging plant for a hardy
border, or make use of its strong colors to perk up a rockery
or gravel garden.

PLANT PROFILE	
HEIGHT 12in (30cm)	
SPREAD 12in (30cm)	
HABIT Dwarf, upright bush	
HARDINESS Borderline hardy	
FLOWERING Summer	

'Tom Thumb'

A LOVELY DWARF FUCHSIA that is perfect for the front of the border, as a miniature hedge, or as a feature plant for a rockery or gravel garden. It is also good in a pot. Surprisingly, such a modern-looking cultivar is, in fact, a golden oldie, having been raised in France as long ago as 1850. Very bushy, compact growth, strong petal color (carmine and purple), and a free-flowering habit that starts early in the season make it hard to beat. One small drawback—the flowers tend to fall prematurely, but since they are produced in such large numbers, this is just a minor detail.

PLANT PROFILE

HEIGHT 6–12in (15–30cm)

SPREAD 6–12in (15–30cm)

HABIT Dwarf, upright bush, self-branching

HARDINESS Z9–11 H12–9

FLOWERING Summer to autumn

'Tom West'

VARIEGATED FOLIAGE IN CERISE, grayish green, and cream is
the main reason why this fuchsia is grown. The strongest
colors appear on young leaves, which can be encouraged by
pinching out the stems regularly. A sunny spot in the garden
will boost the variegation, but avoid strong midday sun or
the cream color will be lost. The single flowers, while not
exceptional, are freely produced and good-sized, enhancing
the overall appearance of the plant. 'Tom West' is a vigorous,
bushy fuchsia that is happy in containers, but wait until the
potting mix is dry before watering to prevent leaf drop.

PLANT PROFILE

HEIGHT 12–24in (30–60cm)

SPREAD 12–24in (30–60cm)

HABIT Lax upright bush, self-branching

HARDINESS Z9–11 H12–9

FLOWERING Summer to first frost

T | 'Trase'

PANACHE IS SOMETHING this fuchsia has in abundance. The small, double flowers are in the useful color combination of carmine and white; coupled with a vigorous, upright, bushy growth habit, it is no wonder this is such a popular cultivar. Given a protective layer of shredded bark to keep out the worst of the winter frosts, it can be left growing outdoors all year in some areas. If you are looking for a dash of red to give lift to an all-white scheme, 'Trase' will fit the bill.

PLANT PROFILE

HEIGHT 18–24in (45–60cm)

SPREAD 18–24in (45–60cm)

HABIT Upright bush, self-branching

HARDINESS Fully hardy

FLOWERING Summer

'Tristesse'

T

EASY TO GROW AND TRAIN, this thoroughly reliable fuchsia has upright, bushy growth and an abundant show of soft-colored flowers. It is an easy one to accommodate in gardens where there is a preponderance of pastel colors. Use it to fill gaps in the front of a border, extend summer annual plans, and soften hot beds of shrieking reds and yellows.

PLANT PROFILE		
HEIGHT 18in (45cm)		
SPREAD 15–18in (38–45cm)		
HABIT Upright bush, self-branching		
HARDINESS Half hardy		
FLOWERING Summer to first frost		

T

'Trumpeter'

WITH ITS LONG, SLENDER FLOWERS, 'Trumpeter' is very
obviously a Triphylla-type fuchsia. Naturally trailing growth
makes it a good choice for a hanging basket, where the rose
red flowers will dangle in clusters like exotic insects from
long, wiry stems. The blooms make a refreshing change from
more conventional fuchsia cultivars. The leaves play their part
too, and are an interesting shade of bluish green. If left to
its own devices, there is a risk that 'Trumpeter' will become
wayward, so start your regimen of pinching out while it is
young and easy to control.

PLANT PROFILE

HEIGHT 9–12in (23–30cm)

SPREAD 12–15in (30–38cm)

HABIT Trailing

HARDINESS Frost tender

FLOWERING Summer

'Voodoo'

V

THE EXCEPTIONALLY LARGE DOUBLE FLOWERS are so plentiful that you may have to support the stems to stop them from splaying out and ruining the neat, upright shape of the plant. 'Voodoo' demands to be treated as a feature plant in a patio container or at the front of the border, and it is also very popular as a cut flower for exotic arrangements.

PLANT PROFILE

HEIGHT 18in (45cm)

SPREAD 15–18in (38–45cm)

HABIT Upright bush, self-branching

HARDINESS Z8–10

FLOWERING Summer to first frost

W '*Walz Jubelteen*'

ONE FOR LOVERS OF PASTEL COLORS, 'Walz Jubelteen' is
a subtle combination of pale pink and pinkish orange. The
small, delicate, single flowers are held facing upward on rather
stiff bushy growth. It was raised in the Netherlands in 1990
by J. H. Waldenmaier, who has introduced many wonderful
modern fuchsias with the prefix 'Walz'. Reliably free-
flowering, use it as a summer bedder or to fill patio containers.

PLANT PROFILE

HEIGHT 18–24in (45–60cm)

SPREAD 18–24in (45–60cm)

HABIT Upright bush,
self-branching

HARDINESS Half hardy

FLOWERING Summer to first frost

'Waveney Gem'

W

WITH EXUBERANT TRAILING STEMS, the best way to grow
'Waveney Gem' is in a hanging basket. However, a lax habit
makes for versatility, and it can be trained as a small standard
or, if given adequate support, will make a loosely shaped,
upright bush. From early summer, the long stems are covered
with elegant white and mauve-pink blooms; flowering
continues unabated until the first frost. Use this informal plant
to soften any hard, unyielding lines in a formal garden, such as
the straight edges of a patio or path.

PLANT PROFILE	
HEIGHT 18in (45cm)	
SPREAD 18–24in (45–60cm)	
HABIT Trailing	
HARDINESS Half hardy	
FLOWERING Summer to first frost	

W | 'Wedding Bells'

'WEDDING BELLS' IS AN ALL-WHITE cultivar with bushy, strong growth. For the brightest white, keep it out of direct sun; however, despite this precaution, it will inevitably take on a pink blush as it matures. It is a useful, all-purpose fuchsia that will make a wonderful contrast with a wide range of colors, especially bold reds and purples. Confusingly, there are several other 'Wedding Bells' on the market, but this one was raised by Dresman in the UK in 1987.

PLANT PROFILE

HEIGHT 15–18in (38–45cm)

SPREAD 15–18in (38–45cm)

HABIT Upright bush

HARDINESS Half hardy

FLOWERING Summer to first frost

'White King'

W

A PARTICULARLY BEAUTIFUL ALL-WHITE fuchsia, 'White King' has large, full flowers with a swirl of upswept sepals and a plump double corolla with softly pleated petals. It also has large foliage and will make a sizable plant. For the best display of trailing stems to fill a hanging basket, start training it early by pinching out the growing tips in spring. Hanging the basket in light dappled shade ensures that the white stands out.

PLANT PROFILE	
HEIGHT 24in (60cm)	
SPREAD 18–24in (45–60cm)	
HABIT Trailing	
HARDINESS Half hardy	
FLOWERING Summer to first frost	

W | ## 'Whiteknights Pearl'

A LOVELY HEDGING FUCHSIA that can be left growing in the border all year in mild regions. It makes a tallish, vigorous bush, well covered in small single flowers. The tube is almost white, the sepals are soft salmon pink, and the corolla is a slightly darker clear pink. The flower color stays true in full sun and looks particularly delicate highlighted against the dark green leaves. 'Whiteknights Pearl' is a shapely bush that will grow well in a large container.

PLANT PROFILE

HEIGHT 36in (90cm)

SPREAD 36in (90cm)

HABIT Upright bush

HARDINESS Fully hardy

FLOWERING Summer to first frost

The publisher would like to thank the following for their kind permission to reproduce their photographs:

a=above; c=center; b=below; l=left; r=right; t=top

6: Harry Smith Collection(c); Brian North (tr); **18:** Four Oaks Nursery; **21:** Photos Horticultural; **26:** Four Oaks Nursery; **27:** Four Oaks Nursery; **31:** Silverdale Nursery; **37:** Four Oaks Nursery; **40:** A-Z Botanical Collection: Anthony Cooper; **41:** Photos Horticultural; **42:** Silverdale Nursery; **43:** Four Oaks Nursery; **46:** Four Oaks Nursery; **50:** Four Oaks Nursery; **51:** Silverdale Nursery; **57:** Four Oaks Nursery; **62:** A-Z Botanical Collection: Tony Wood; **66:** Photos Horticultural; **69:** A-Z Botanical Collection: Mike Danson; **72:** Four Oaks Nursery; **76:** Four Oaks Nursery; **78:** A-Z Botanical Collection: M.P.Land; **79:** Photos Horticultural; **84:** A-Z Botanical Collection: Bob Gibbons; **87:** A-Z Botanical Collection: Mike Danson; **91:** Four Oaks Nursery; **93:** A-Z Botanical Collection: Adrian Thomas; **98:** Four Oaks Nursery; **102:** A-Z Botanical Collection: Ian Vernon; **105:** Four Oaks Nursery; **109:** Four Oaks Nursery; **110:** Four Oaks Nursery; **116:** Photos Horticultural; **122:** A-Z Botanical Collection: Tony Wood; **125:** Proven Winners Nurser; **126:** Silverdale Nursery: Peter Anderson; **128:** Silverdale Nursery; **137:** Four Oaks Nursery; **140:** Silverdale Nursery; **148:** Four Oaks Nursery; **149:** Four Oaks Nursery; **150:** Silverdale Nursery; **151:** Four Oaks Nursery; **154:** Harry Smith Collection; **155:** A-Z Botanical Collection: Adrian Thomas; **156:** Four Oaks Nursery; **162:** Four Oaks Nursery; **172:** A-Z Botanical Collection; **177:** Four Oaks Nursery; **187:** Silverdale Nursery; **189:** Harry Smith Collection; **191:** Proven Winners Nursery;: **191:** Harry Smith Collection; **194:** Silverdale Nursery; **196:** Four Oaks Nursery; **199:** Four Oaks Nursery; **200:** Four Oaks Nursery; **210:** Four Oaks Nursery; **212:** A-Z Botanical Collection: Dan Sams; **216:** Four Oaks Nursery; **217:** A-Z Botanical Collection: Ian Gowland;. **219:** Harry Smith Collection; **221:** Harry Smith Collection; **222:** Harry Smith Collection; **225:** Four Oaks Nursery; **226:** Silverdale Nursery; **228:** Four Oaks Nursery; **229:** Four Oaks Nursery; **233:** Four Oaks Nursery; **235:** Four Oaks Nursery; **236:** Four Oaks Nursery; **237:** Four Oaks Nursery; **239:** Silverdale Nursery; **241:** Harry Smith Collection; **242:** Four Oaks Nursery; **257:** Silverdale Nursery; **260:** Four Oaks Nursery; **261:** A-Z Botanical Collection: Adrian Thomas; **262:** Four Oaks Nursery; **265:** Four Oaks Nursery; **269:** Four Oaks Nursery; **270:** Silverdale Nursery; **274:** Photos Horticultural; **275:** Harry Smith Collection; **276:** Four Oaks Nursery; **277:** Four Oaks Nursery; **278:** Harry Smith Collection; **279:** Four Oaks Nursery; **280:** Four Oaks Nursery; **282:** Four Oaks Nursery; **283:** Harry Smith Collection; **287:** Four Oaks Nursery; **288:** A-Z Botanical Collection: W.D.Monks; **291:** Four Oaks Nursery; **292:** Harry Smith Collection; **294:** Four Oaks Nursery; **297:** Four Oaks Nursery; **307:** Four Oaks Nursery; **310:** A-Z Botanical Collection: Mrs. W. Monks; **311:** A-Z Botanical Collection: Archie Young; **314:** Four Oaks Nursery; **316:** Four Oaks Nursery (bl); **317:** Four Oaks Nursery (bl); **318:** Photos Horticultural (bl).

All other images © Dorling Kindersley.

For further information see:
www.dkimages.com

Dorling Kindersley would also like to thank the following:
Helen Fewster and Letitia Luff for their editorial assistance; and Archie Clapton in Media Resources.

Brynawel Fuchsia & Garden Center
Sully Road, Penarth CF64 2TR
South Wales, UK
Tel: (02920) 702660
www.brynawelgardencentre.co.uk

The Duchy of Cornwall Nursery
Cott Road, Lostwithiel
Cornwall PL22 0HW
Tel: (01208) 872668
www.duchyofcornwallnursery.co.uk

Fuchsia World
21 Pye Green Road
Hednesford Staffordshire WS12 4LP
Tel: (01543) 422394

Riverside Fuchsias & Nursery
R/O Ernest Dee
Main Road
Sutton-at-hone, Dartford
Kent DA4 9HQ
Tel: (01322) 863891

Silver Dale Nurseries
Shute Lane, Combe Martin
Devon EX34 0HT
Tel: (01271) 882539
Email: silverdale.nurseries@virgin.net

Skagit Valley Gardens
1695 Peter Johnson Road
Mt. Vernon, WA
Tel: (360) 424-6760

Tiedemann Nurseries
4707 Cherryvale Avenue
Soquel, CA 95073-9553
Tel: (831) 475-5996

Weidner's Gardens
695 Normandy Road
Encinitas, CA 92024-1806
Tel: (760) 436-5326

Wileywood Nursery
17414 Bothell-Everett Highway
Mill Creek, WA 98012
Tel: (425) 481-9768

BRITISH SUPPLIERS:
(Many of these can supply fuchsias
via mail-order, including rare cultivars
unavailable in the US.)

Arcadia Nurseries
Brass Castle Lane
Nunthorpe, Middlesbrough
Cleveland TS8 9EB
(01642) 310782
www.arcadianurseries.co.uk

The Earthworks
8034 SE 248th
Covington, WA 98042
Tel: (253) 631-8283
www.fuchsias.net

Fuchsiarama
3201 N Highway 1
Fort Bragg, CA 95437-9535
Tel: (707) 964-0429

Half Moon Bay Nursery
1691 San Mateo Rd.
Half Moon Bay, CA 94019
Tel: (650) 726-0881

Joy Creek Nursery
20300 NW Watson Road
Scappoose, OR 97056
Tel: (503) 543-7474

Pearson's Nursery
26626 132nd Avnue SE
Kent, WA 98042
Tel: (253) 631-3743

Regine's Fuchsia Garden
32531 Rhoda Lane
Fort Bragg, CA 95437
Tel: (707) 964 0183

Fuchsia suppliers

You should find many of the fuchsias in this book at garden centers, but for more unusual varieties, try contacting these specialist nurseries:

Antonelli Brothers Nursery
2545 Capitola Road
Santa Cruz, CA 95062
Tel: (831) 475-5222
antnelli.infopoint.com

Barnhaven Gardens
1920 Landing Road
Mt. Vernon, WA
Tel: (360) 466-5805

D & B Fuchsia Nursery
14520 NE 74th Street
Vancouver, WA 98682
www.fuchsialand.com

Delta Farm & Nursery
3925 North Delta Highway
Eugene, OR 97408
Tel: (541) 485-2992
www.deltafarm.com

'Zulu King'

THE DARK RED AND PURPLE FLOWERS of this cultivar won't fade with age, and retain their rich deep tones until they fall. Growth is spreading, with long, trailing stems that are ideally suited to a hanging basket. However, it will also look good in a gravel garden, where the dark green foliage will stand out well against the pale-colored stones.

PLANT PROFILE	
HEIGHT 12–15in (30–38cm)	
SPREAD 24–36in (60–90cm)	
HABIT Trailing	
HARDINESS Half hardy	
FLOWERING Summer to first frost	

'Winston Churchill'

A RELIABLE AND PROLIFIC FLOWERER, this wonderful cultivar makes a luxurious summer bedding plant. However, it is more deserving of a place of honor in an ornamental planter, either grown as a bush or trained as a standard. The medium-sized, petal-packed double flowers come in a striking blend of pink and lavender purple. Take plenty of cuttings each year, since this fuchsia can be difficult to overwinter.

PLANT PROFILE

HEIGHT 18–30in (45–75cm)

SPREAD 18–30in (45–75cm)

HABIT Upright bush, self-branching

HARDINESS Half hardy

FLOWERING Summer to first frost

W

'White Spider'

ONE GLANCE AT THE SEPALS and you'll see how this fuchsia got its name. Although tinged with pink rather than pure white, they are long and slender and curl above the white corolla. This pretty cultivar has so many things going for it that you can forgive the unfortunate name. Growth is vigorous and upright (it makes a good standard) and from early summer it is very free-flowering. Plant it against a dark background to highlight the delicate flowers.

PLANT PROFILE	
HEIGHT	18–24in (45–60cm)
SPREAD	12–15in (30–38cm)
HABIT	Upright bush
HARDINESS	Half hardy
FLOWERING	Summer to first frost